SACRED STACKS

The Higher Purpose of Libraries and Librarianship

NANCY KALIKOW MAXWELL

AMERICAN LIBRARY ASSOCIATION
Chicago   2006

While extensive effort has gone into ensuring the reliability of information appearing in this book, the publisher makes no warranty, express or implied, on the accuracy or reliability of the information, and does not assume and hereby disclaims any liability to any person for any loss or damage caused by errors or omissions in this publication.

Printed on 50-pound white offset, a pH-neutral stock, and bound in 10-point cover stock by Batson Printing.

The paper used in this publication meets the minimum requirements of American National Standard for Information Sciences—Permanence of Paper for Printed Library Materials, ANSI Z39.48-1992. ∞

Library of Congress Cataloging-in-Publication Data

Maxwell, Nancy Kalikow.
    Sacred stacks : the higher purpose of libraries and librarianship / Nancy Kalikow Maxwell.
      p.   cm.
    Includes bibliographical references and index.
    ISBN 0-8389-0917-5
    1. Libraries—Religious aspects. 2. Libraries and society. 3. Libraries—Aims and objectives. 4. Books and reading—Religious aspects. 5. Library science—Philosophy. I. Title.

    Z716.4M37 2006
    027—dc22   2006000573

Printed in the United States of America

10 09 08 07 06   5 4 3 2 1

To the memory of my father,
Albert Kalikow,
1918–2004.
He would have been so proud.

Contents

Preface

Hurrying to a meeting on the campus of a Catholic college where I worked, I nearly missed seeing the approaching student. "Hi, Sister," he said. "Thanks so much for helping me in the library. My paper came out great."

Did he just call me "Sister"? I thought. I quickly dismissed his salutation. I must have heard him wrong.

The second time it happened, I knew my ears were functioning fine. After I delivered a litany of unresolved building problems to the new facilities manager, he said, "Let's go take a look and see what we can do about some of these." Reaching the door, he waved me on and said, "After you, Sister."

This time I knew I had heard correctly.

"I'm not a Sister," I laughed. "As a matter of fact, I'm Jewish."

A different sort of misidentification led to an epiphany so profound I ended up writing this book about it. Before a campuswide meeting, the department chair, who was also a nun, circled the room introducing a new faculty member she had in tow. When she reached me, I braced myself for the "Sister Nancy" moniker. Instead, I heard, "Allow me to introduce you to our librarian, Nancy Maxwell. She ministers in the library."

I am definitely getting my hearing checked, I thought. She just said I "minister." I am a librarian. I don't minister.

Or do I? The introduction led me to question whether my chosen profession was in some way a spiritual vocation. Countless times I have heard librarians refer to their professional choice as a "calling." Given the common confusion of librarians and nuns, perhaps other similarities exist between those two populations.

It took an overheard conversation between two reference librarians finally to reveal to me the intrinsic spiritual dimension of my chosen profession. One of the reference librarians (who like the department chair was also a nun) was speaking to another librarian. Though I did not know the original topic under discussion, I overheard the nun saying, "Everything I do is an offering up to God."

The librarian she was addressing was known to be a feisty, radically non-religious person, so it was surprising when she responded: "I know exactly what you mean. I feel the same way. I can't describe it, because I'm not sure I even believe in God. But at the reference desk, I feel like I am offering my work up to Something or Somebody beyond myself." After an uncharacteristic moment of silence, she added, "In the library I feel I am serving some greater purpose."

This book is about that "greater purpose" of libraries rarely discussed, or even acknowledged. And no wonder. It is difficult to see the library's higher aspects when you spend the day clearing paper jams, refereeing fights over computers, and yelling at people to quiet their cell phones. And those are the good days. On the bad days librarians spend their time defending their profession altogether, crafting counterarguments to that oft-heard phrase, "It's all on the Internet." From the digitization of library resources to the onslaught of web-based information, librarians are on the defensive. Many librarians worry that our print collections, along with ourselves, will soon no longer be needed.

But we need not worry. As I discuss in this book, librarians serve a higher purpose that no amount of digitization or computerization can ever replace. Decades ago dire predictions abounded that religion was obsolete, yet today religions continue and thrive. Likewise, many have issued death knells for libraries. Yet libraries, too, have remained. This book argues that libraries have survived, and will continue to thrive in the future, because they fulfill eternal needs for people. Like clergy and members of religious orders, librarians hold a sacred profession, albeit one performed in a secular setting. For an explanation of this thesis, come with Sister Nancy as we head into the *Sacred Stacks* of the library.

Acknowledgments

One of the central tenets of this book is that, no matter how long human life expectancy extends in the future, it will never come close to that of libraries. Even if people come to live for hundreds of years, they will never outlive libraries. The library as an institution will go on forever.

The image of some anonymous person of the future stumbling upon this book on a dusty shelf in a library kept me plugging away at this writing. Seeing them flip to the first pages of this missive also drives the list included on this page. By choosing to mention the following people, I am granting to them a portion of imagined immortality.

Writing this book turned out to be much more difficult than expected. Though I stayed motivated by my imagined future readers, I also needed—as the song has it—a little help from my friends. (Note to future readers: that comes from a lovely little Beatles song. A librarian of the future can help you locate the tune.) Throughout the arduous process of writing, I was blessed with the help, support, guidance, and patience of many. To each, I offer my sincere appreciation, along with this bit of eternal recognition. Like me, now each of you can revel in the idea of a person someday in the future finding this book, seeing this reference, and knowing you were helpful. What better way is there to be remembered?

Eternal thanks to

> The steadfast members of the Florida Center for the Book Tuesday Evening Critique Group, who heard more of this book than they wanted. Every page is better, thanks to group leader Carole Lytle, Sue Alspach, Marge Bowman, Jackie Culver, Kathleen Dixon Donnelly, Leslie Goulet, Pat Gray, Natasha Grinberg, Arden Kahlo, Andrew Kingston, Alyce Marshall, Jack Nease, Nadine Seide, and Deborah Sharp.

Dr. Celia Suarez, for being a great boss and doing all she could to support this writing. Special thanks to every member of the staff of Miami Dade College North Campus Library.

The faculty and staff of Barry University's Monsignor William Barry Memorial Library and Department of Theology and Philosophy, who provided the impetus and insights needed for this book.

Leonard Kniffel, Beverly Goldberg, and Pamela Goodes at *American Libraries* for helping spread the word about this book.

Patrick Hogan, Emily Moroni, Russell Harper, and all the wonderful staff of ALA Editions, who patiently worked with me to take this from idea to book. I was blessed to have you working on this book, and I don't use that word lightly.

A special expression of love and affection to my mother, Betty Kalikow; sister, Barbara Kalikow Schwartz; brother, Harvey Kalikow; cousin, Judy Mesch; and all their spouses and kids. We made it through a difficult time. You all helped me keep going just by asking, "How's the book coming?"

And of course, to my husband, Rod, and daughter, Amanda, who suffered through every page with me. At last this book is done. Thanks for being with me throughout. I am literally eternally grateful.

CHAPTER ONE

Libraries as Sacred, Secular Intitutions

*A*s reference librarians are well aware, library patrons come in spurts. Sometimes you sit for hours without one person approaching you, and then out of nowhere seven people appear at once. Whenever lines formed in front of me at the reference desk, I would frantically try to serve them all at once. While jotting down a call number for the first person, I would point to the new book section for the next. Mouthing the words "in a minute" to one, I would nod at another while I dialed the phone to request immediate backup help. Amid the flurry of activity, I would say to myself, *Calm down, Nancy. Remember, this is a library, not a hospital. No one is going to die here.*

Actually, I did once face a life-or-death issue at the reference desk, but it came via the telephone rather than in person. The caller had to know what compound would put out a chemical fire that had broken out in a janitor's closet. Recognizing the dire nature of the query, I suggested the caller hang up and immediately call the fire department. I realized just how critical the situation was when the voice on the phone said, "This *is* the fire department."

1

Though most calls to the library do not involve putting out fires, the library is critical for its users. Library science professor Wayne A. Wiegand claims librarians spend too much time discussing "the user in the library" when they should instead focus on "the library in the life of our users."[1] *Sacred Stacks* answers his plea by discussing not users' needs but users' souls. Rarely do librarians think about their profession in terms of souls. Online resources, information literacy, instructional assessment, user needs: these are concepts ALA Editions publishes books about and librarians discuss at library conferences. But people use libraries on a level far more profound. Behind their requests for the latest Stephen King novel or Abraham Lincoln's birth date lies significance they may not even be aware of. When one looks deeply, library use can be seen as spiritual, sacred, sometimes even heavenly.

LIBRARIES AS HEAVEN

Libraries are heavenly institutions. I don't say that just because I'm a librarian. Others who do not share my profession have said as much. "I have always imagined Paradise as a kind of library," said author Jorge Luis Borges. The concept of heavenly books and writings are found among many ancient peoples.[2] In Babylonian literature the gods possessed "tablets of destiny." Divine books are mentioned in several places in the Bible, with later texts describing a pair of angels as the keepers of the Books.[3]

For others heaven is not "The Great Library in the Sky" but rather is located in libraries here on earth. In the remake of the movie *City of Angels*, Meg Ryan meets her personal guardian angel—in the form of Nicolas Cage—in the stacks of the Los Angeles Public Library. Like his fellow angels, Cage chooses the library as his earthly haunt because all knowledge resides there, all languages are spoken, and communication travels—like the angels themselves—at the speed of thought.

Perhaps the finest reference to divine libraries was directed, not at the institution, but at the people who work there. "Librarians," said an acquaintance upon learning my profession, "are God's gift to mankind." When I laughed at her suggestion, she added, "I'm not kidding. Honestly, I think they are."

"God's gift." "Heaven on earth." "Angels in the stacks." Libraries lend themselves to ethereal images that would be ridiculous for other venues and professions. How often are hardware stores or post offices pictured as heavenly? I cannot ever recall hearing lawyers characterized as gifts from God.

References to holy insurance offices or dry cleaners strike us as funny because they are so incongruous. Yet something about the nature of libraries seems spiritual. What is it, this book asks, that makes libraries seem sublime?

Most people think of religious library use as reading religious books or using a religion-affiliated library. This book does not refer to either of these uses. Rather, this book addresses the hidden religious aspects of the nonreligious use of secular libraries.

I am well aware that librarians may take exception to referring to their profession as a religious activity. Unless they work in a religious institution or with a collection of religious materials, many librarians believe their religious life—if they have one at all—is completely separate from their professional life. I know I did. As the only Jew employed in a Catholic university library—perhaps because of this—I was keenly aware that I was performing a secular function in the library. Dispensing information and helping students were secular, even if elsewhere on campus specifically religious activities were taking place. I, like my professional colleagues, prided myself on my ability to assist objectively all who came to me for help, regardless of the religious or secular nature of their request.

It was not until I studied religions academically through a graduate theology program that the premise of this book was revealed. While working at a Catholic university, I obtained a master's degree in Catholic theology (thanks to their free employee tuition benefit). With the conferral of this degree, I earned the distinction of being the only Jew to graduate from the college's Catholic religious graduate program.[4] But along with an interesting twist in my biography, I gained an understanding of the elements that compose religions in general. By constantly comparing two religions, I not only learned about their similarities and differences but gained insight into the components that make up a religion.

I soon realized that many religion-like features are present in the secular setting of the library. As I discuss in this book, aspects of theology, cosmological order, salvation—all religious concepts—can be located in the secular setting of the library. What is more, many religious activities—the search for immortality, fellowship, sanctuary, and purpose—can be seen every day in library usage.

SACRED AND SECULAR BLURRING

Imagining religion-like aspects in a secular setting such as the library would have been unthinkable in years past. In the "good old days," what you did in church was religious and what happened outside was secular. But now the two worlds are colliding, blending, and mixing in ways unfathomable to previous generations. What is "religious" is now seen everywhere, not just in church. Religious institutions are adopting many of the accoutrements—and some fear the principles—of the secular world, while religious seekers are venturing beyond the confines of their houses of worship to find meaning and purpose in their lives.

A comment made by a member of my writers group encapsulated this changed attitude: "In my church we don't believe in the sacred," she said.

I found it more than a little strange that her Christian denomination would lack that central element. Though I knew her to be an intelligent woman, I doubted that she understood her religion well enough to make such a claim. But as she continued with her explanation, I quickly realized I had underestimated her theological understanding: "In my church we think everything is sacred. There is not really a difference between what is secular and what is sacred. We look at everything you do or say as holy."

To see a physical manifestation of the blurring of sacred and secular, one need look no farther than a newly constructed church building. New houses of worship—especially what are called megachurches—now resemble entertainment centers more than religious sanctuaries. State-of-the-art projection and sound systems create the appearance of a sophisticated theater, or even a rock concert hall.

Beyond the look of the building, religious institutions employ the techniques of the secular world, especially those of business. Targeted marketing, ad campaigns, direct-mail appeals are all standard practices of many American religions. Evaluations of clergy's sermons—an appalling notion just a few generations ago—are common among several denominations.

These responses, which have occurred to a certain extent within all American religions, are fascinating, though beyond the scope that can be explored here. But a brief explanation of why sacred and secular intermingling has occurred may be useful. One of the most prevalent, and I believe compelling, explanations of the collapse of the religious and nonreligious spheres can be found in a sea change in the contemporary American religious scene. This fundamental shift can be summarized with the three words below.

SPIRITUAL, NOT RELIGIOUS

For most of U.S. history, the predominant religion in this country was Protestantism, with Catholicism representing the largest single denomination. But today neither of these religious affiliations can claim dominance; rather, "spiritual, but not religious" is the description most often heard by religion scholars as the characterization of Americans' faith.[5]

Though people freely describe themselves as "spiritual, but not religious," rarely can they articulate what the assignation means. It has wryly been posited that baby boomers invented the phrase so they could enjoy the benefits of religion without organized religion getting in the way.

Within the academic religion community, oceans of ink and mountains of paper have been spent trying to pinpoint the tenets of the phrase. A summary of these discussions is beyond the scope of this work. For this purpose "spiritual, but not religious" can be taken to mean experiencing a religious sentiment or enacting a sacred ritual beyond the confines of a specific religious denomination. Though the belief or practice may be grounded in a religious tradition, the "spiritual, but not religious" person sees personal choice, rather than religious obligation, as his or her prime motivator.

One of the reasons Americans feel free to describe themselves as "spiritual, but not religious" is that religion in America has gone from being "ascribed" to "achieved." People have granted to themselves the freedom to define what, if any, religion they will practice. No longer are individuals limited to the religion they were born into. Doctrine, church attendance, denominational loyalty, and a host of religious concepts that were the cornerstones of faith years ago hold little sway for most people today. Beginning in the 1970s, religion increasingly became a chosen identity that was not often the same as the religious identity of one's parents or one's upbringing. Embracing a religion is now looked upon as an opportunity to choose, much like other consumer selections. You can choose Coke or Pepsi, Nike or Reebok. Why not Buddhism or Judaism? Some scholars even refer to the religious landscape as the "spiritual marketplace."[6]

An astounding number of people are exercising their newfound religious freedom by switching religions. In 1955 only 4 percent of Americans switched from the religion of their childhood to another faith. Now nearly one in three changes religions. Catholics, Jews, and Mormons still have the lowest switching rates, though Catholics have a tendency to leave and come back, while Jews change denominations within Judaism. Remarkably, one survey found more than half of pastors were serving in a ministry other than the one of their seminary training.[7]

Others choose to stay within their faith tradition but insist that it change to meet their personal spiritual needs. Sometimes these demands are different, or even at odds, with the religious tradition.

Individuals have freed themselves not only from institutional commit-
ments but also from religious dogma. Before "spiritual, but not religious" became the dominant American faith, belief in a religious dogma was often a key
component of a "religious" person. However, even this traditional component
of religion no longer yields meaning in many people's search for religion. For
instance, within Christianity one fundamental doctrine has been a belief in a
divine, saving Jesus. Boston University's Stephen Prothero has noted that
even this basic tenet is changing. American Christians have gradually liberated
Jesus from divinity and dogma, "turning Jesus into more of a Dalai Lama, an
admirable kind of guy."[8]

Even in fundamentalist, evangelical churches one will not find an expected
unified belief. In one study of such congregations, a devout church member
admitted, "We call ourselves Christian, but we don't know what we believe."
Another study revealed that "even Calvinists have beliefs that differ from
Calvinist dogma dictates." One sociologist found that in a conservative
Christian church that opposed a gay-rights referendum the congregants were
far less certain of themselves and their beliefs and were much more fractious
than she expected.[9]

"Heinz 57 church" is how one pastor characterized the variety of doc-
trines held by his parishioners. Others have coined the term "Golden Rule
Christians" to refer to those who adhere to a broad ethical system rather than
a traditional doctrinal view of their faith. For many Reform Jews, Judaism is
not so much a doctrinal religion as it is an ethical system.

A survey of young Catholics found that significant numbers of them "no
longer see the Roman Catholic Church as unique or essential, the pope as necessary, the Church's structures as important, or tradition as a source of objec-
tive truth. A minority of Catholics believes the Catholic Church is the one
true church."[10]

Though 96 percent of Americans believe in God, or a universal spirit,
most regard religious teachings more as suggestions than commandments.[11]
Some scholars believe this changing attitude toward doctrine has been accompanied—or perhaps caused by—the rise in multicultural acceptance. If all cultures are meritorious, so are their religions. No longer do white Anglo-Saxon
Protestants have hegemony, either culturally or religiously. But without any
one group taking dominance, there is no recognized source of authority for
doctrine or other aspects of religion.

Loosened from its moorings of doctrinal or institutional loyalty, religion
in America has evolved (or devolved) into embracing values that give meaning
to one's life. Nowhere is this more obvious than in the popular sociological

term "Sheilaism." Encapsulating what Alan Wolfe calls the "populistic, personalistic and anti-institutional" American view of religion, Sheilaism is the personal creation of one's religion. The term derives from a young nurse, Sheila Larson, who was interviewed about her religious beliefs for the book *Habits of the Heart*.[12] Explaining that she made up her own religion, she described her religious stance by saying, "I believe in God. I'm not a religious fanatic. I can't remember the last time I went to church," but she did adhere to a faith that she had dubbed "'Sheilaism,' just my own little voice." Like so many people today, she would pick and choose religious tenets and practices that resonated personally, patching them together into her own unifying religious outlook. "Sheilaism" has come to mean the process many Americans use to describe their faith by substituting their own name for hers.

The personal resonance of religion is especially important to members of Generation X. For many in this age group the word "religion" carries negative connotations, though they remain open to discovering what they define as spirituality.[13] Whether located within or without a church setting, they continue to search for personal authenticity and meaning.

But it is not only younger Americans who are exploring personal faith. Both young and old can be found among what sociologist Robert Wuthnow and others have dubbed religious "seekers" as opposed to "dwellers."[14] Especially in unsettled times as we are experiencing now, people "seek" spirituality based on personal meaning rather than "dwell" in a religious place or practice that provides familiarity, habit, and security. Even older, died-in-the-wool Catholics find the personal amorphous experience of spirituality important. When members of this demographic group were asked their reason for attending Mass, only 20 percent of Catholics said they came to church to receive the sacraments; 37 percent were seeking "the *feeling* of meditating and communicating with God."[15]

SECULAR SPIRITUAL SPHERES

Some social scientists theorize that the winners from the diffusion of religious sentiment are secular settings. Anthropologist Mircea Eliade claims that everyone as a member of the human race has specifically religious needs.[16] Without even recognizing them, these needs find a way into each person's life. In this "zero-sum game," when you subtract religious energies from one place, those energies immediately flow into another.[17] Since organized religion is losing dominance in the "meaning-seeking" venue, others must be gaining.

Though people imbue secular venues with religious meaning, this transfer is often unrecognized. As one scholar put it, sacred aspects revealed in the profane (nonsacred) world are often ignored, camouflaged, or degraded, but that does not mean they do not exist.[18] Because they are hidden, revealing secular milieus laden with religious meaning has become an interesting—and often amusing—scholarly pursuit. Areas that have been plumbed for religious meaning are as plentiful and fanciful as the scholars who study them.[19]

Examples of Sacred, Secular Venues

Sports was one of the first and most prevalent secular arenas (no pun intended) where scholars saw religious themes played out.[20] "Golf is his religion" is an abbreviated way of seeing sports as sacred. In my house, Sunday afternoon has been dubbed my husband's football *Shabbos* (Sabbath), because his adherence to the game-watching ritual rivals the religious practice of even the most orthodox Jew. "Religiosport" is a recently coined term that sees stadiums as shrines, the games as services, chants as rituals, and highly paid athletes as priests.[21] The reemergence of football players from the tunnel to the playing field after halftime has been likened to symbolic death and rebirth. The ritual pouring of champagne over the heads of winning team members is reminiscent of the baptismal ceremony.

In our consumer-based culture, the spending, saving, and investing of money have earned religious interpretations. In an imaginative *Atlantic Monthly* article, Harvey Cox found theological parallels in the stock market. God's wrath and the Dow Jones Industrials inexplicably ebb and flow despite all mortal attempts at control. Schlepping the kids to Disney World has been compared to an obligatory religious pilgrimage. Shopping malls can be seen as sacred venues. Escalators deliver the righteous to a climate-controlled, consumer heaven much like the biblical ladder transported Jacob skyward. Columnist David Brooks called the cash register a gateway to paradise. Through purchases people hope to fulfill their lofty ideals.[22]

The consumption (or avoidance of) certain foods also yields a delicious cornucopia of religious meaning. For instance, the avoidance of "sinful" desserts has been seen as a pathway to salvation, while tolerating a meal of tasteless tofu can be seen as virtuous self-sacrifice. One prominent religious scholar wrote an entire book chapter on the religious significance of southern barbecue, finding sacrifice, communion, and religious fellowship in his plate of spareribs. This dish represented for him the culinary resolution of the intercultural conflict between competing religious and secular cultures. In an excellent example of a mundane pop culture element taking on greater meaning, McDonald's founder Ray Kroc said, "The French fry became almost sacrosanct to me, its preparation a ritual to be followed religiously."[23]

The world of entertainment has produced more than its share of hidden religious meaning. Television talk shows substitute for religious confession. *Star Wars, Star Trek*, and movie westerns replay the religious themes of good versus evil.[24] *The Wizard of Oz* inspired an entire book on the movie's religious themes of origin, destiny, identity, and cosmology. Especially amusing for this Kansas native was that book's assertion that what makes Dorothy religious is her persistent belief in Oz and that joy is possible "even in Kansas."[25]

Submerged religious impulses have been identified in the cycle of American secular holidays and rituals. Memorial Day, Veteran's Day, and the Fourth of July all evoke the memory and sacrifice of ancestors found in religion. Thanksgiving is the most obvious religion-like holiday, though exactly who or what is being thanked is never specified. Visiting national shrines and monuments such as Plymouth Rock and the Gettysburg battlefield also evokes an emotional impact resembling a religious experience. Some believe the Super Bowl has become a secular religious festival.

Religious underpinnings can also be seen in the American value system. In the book *American Beliefs*, a University of Arizona professor identified four sets of ideals that "keep a big country and a diverse people united." Librarians especially should be able to see the relevance of the following selected American beliefs within the library context:

1. Primary beliefs that everyone must work and must benefit from their work.
2. Immigrant beliefs that improvement is possible and opportunities must be imagined.
3. Frontier beliefs that each person is responsible for his or her own well-being, that helping others helps yourself, and that progress requires organization.
4. Religious and moral beliefs that doing what is right is necessary for happiness and that God gave us all the same birthrights.[26]

The work environment is a logical location for religion to "leak into." Not only is work the source of identity for many people, it also consumes the most daily waking hours in many people's lives. David Brooks has noted that many people end up in a job and "after a while they get absorbed in that world, gradually coming to feel they have found their place in the cosmos."[27] Indeed, Reinhold Niebuhr posited a seemingly ingrained tendency to identify what we do with God's work.[28] "Toil is liturgical, work is worship," observed the author of *The Man Nobody Knows*, one of the first books to try to unite the divide between work and religion.[29]

Library as Sacred, Secular Venue

If the mall and a baseball stadium can be seen as hidden religious venues, surely libraries can as well. Matthew Arnold once said, "In the absence of faith in transcendental religion, poetry may have to do."[30] Libraries, too, have often been referred to in spiritual terms. In the remainder of this book I discuss other religion-like aspects of library use. Similarities between the roles of librarians and members of the clergy are the subject of chapter 2. I review the central role of librarians and catalogers in ordering and opening the world of knowledge in chapter 3. In chapter 4 we see how eternal life is sought through association with the permanence of the library, in chapter 5 how self-improvement has become the modern method of redemption and deliverance. Chapters 6 and 7 show how libraries, like houses of worship, create communities while paradoxically providing sanctuary from them. I discuss the methods children's librarians use to guarantee the continuation of the written cultural legacy in chapter 8 and conclude in chapter 9 with the implications of all these religious similarities.

CONTEMPORARY THEOLOGY

Underpinning this discussion of libraries as sacred, secular institutions is a redefined vision of God. I am reluctant to enter into a discussion of theology in a text about libraries and librarianship, but it seems essential. As William F. Buckley noted, "If you mention God once at a dinner party in New York, you'll be greeted with silence. Twice, you will never be invited back."[31] People are uncomfortable talking about God in public, even though 96 percent of Americans say they believe in some sort of higher power. Indeed, Americans believe in God at rates well above those of all comparable nations. Fifty-eight percent of Americans say their belief in God is very important to their lives, compared to 12 percent of the French and 19 percent of the British. Perhaps revealing of their positive attitude in general, 86 percent of Americans believe in heaven, twice the German percentage.[32] Only 5 percent tell researchers they are atheist or agnostic. I would venture to guess that even some of them surreptitiously communicate with God in hospital waiting rooms As the old adage goes, there are no atheists in foxholes, or—as one of my personal favorites has it—as long as there are math tests, there will be prayer in school.

Though people don't want to talk about God in public, they are secretly fascinated by the subject. Bill Moyers witnessed a firsthand demonstration of this fact when he proposed a public television series called the *Genesis Project*, an interfaith discussion of the first book of the Old Testament. The goal of the series, which included seven religion experts from different faiths, was to encourage Americans to engage in serious conversation about deeply felt subjects—to challenge, teach, and learn from each other. Initially Moyers had a hard time selling the idea. He was repeatedly told that Americans don't want to hear "God-talk" on television. Conventional wisdom had it that people instinctively turned off when they heard any combination of God and television, assuming this mix meant someone was trying to sell them something or put something over on them. Moyers persevered and was rewarded with the most successful program he had ever produced for television. Not only did people watch the program, they gathered in homes, churches, and community centers to discuss the topic. It is estimated that a million people watched and discussed the program. "God-talk" was not only happening but thriving.[33]

One explanation of the success of the *Genesis Project* is that, by presenting theology in an intelligent, thought-provoking style, the program allowed people to acknowledge and discuss their confusion about the subject of God. Millions are wrestling with God—to use the appropriate biblical term for the activity—attempting to replace the Old Man in the Clouds with a more meaningful contemporary image.

Contemporary confusion about God crosses religious lines. Jews are closely allied with God in the public imagination because of their historical dedication to the Torah (Old Testament) and personal relationship with God, as depicted by Tevye in *Fiddler on the Roof.* Religion scholar Alan Wolfe found, however, that American Jews express doubts on matters of theology at levels Christians would most likely consider of crisis proportions. Only 50 percent of Jews agreed that God revealed the Torah, and many do not lend much credence to the God described in their prayer books. That God is too commanding, too particularistic, "too 'Jewish,'" is how one respondent put it. When Jews talk about "religious Jews" they are usually referring to ritual practices rather than to theological dedication. It is not that Jews are atheistic, or even agnostic, but rather "atheological." As sociologist Jonathan Woocher explains, the concept of God plays a less significant role than other issues such as the unity and mutual responsibility of the Jewish people, values, charity, and tradition.[34]

Even Christians are unclear about the exact parameters of their God. Though many Christians passionately believe in God, they cannot tell others all that much about the God in which they believe. Uncertainty about theological tenets is certainly nothing new for American religions. Religion scholar Stephen Prothero claims that by the 1800s Americans increasingly came to view theology as a distraction from true religion. Across diverse religious communities, religions have rejected the authority of ministers, the veracity of creeds, and the importance of theology.[35]

Though many say theology is unimportant to them, they still seek God, even though they don't realize that's what they are doing. Religion scholar Amanda Porterfield argues that many Americans are paradoxically trying to bring God down to earth.[36] One of the problems with traditional images of God is that they usually invoke a supernatural, otherworldly being.

Defining God, like defining religion, can be extremely difficult, if not impossible. Some scholars have given up such an attempt, acknowledging that the term is too complex and imprecise. As with art, people cannot articulate exactly what they mean by the term, but they know it when they see it. Or, more accurately, they know it when they feel it.

Historically, various attempts have been made to define God, most often by listing divine attributes. Classical Christianity defined God as being omnipotent (possessing all powers), omniscient (having all knowledge), and omnipresent (existing everywhere). Instead of compiling laundry lists of God's characteristics, other religions and definitions of God focus on the human experience of God. When viewed through this perspective, God becomes that which is reflected back when people lose themselves in something beyond themselves, experience a feeling of holiness, or commune with something permanent that provides a sense of meaning and completeness.

IMAGINING A LIBRARY GOD

If libraries can easily be imagined as heavenly, perhaps some form of God can also be pictured dwelling within the library. For some, locating a correct metaphor to speak of a library-dwelling God may be difficult. Others may find the notion offensive, even bordering on blasphemy. I mean no offense by these references and in no way wish to denigrate any religious notions of the divine. Rather, the following are offered as examples of sacred aspects of library use that could explain why people experience libraries on a higher plane than other secular places.

Wisdom God

Libraries are perfect examples of God imagined as wisdom. For the ancient Greeks, she—and wisdom was imagined as feminine—was named Sophia, roaming the streets dispensing her knowledge to the world. The biblical book of Ecclesiastes likens this God of Wisdom to Torah. Interpreted broadly, Torah was not limited to the content of the sacred scriptures but referred to the pathway to truth, knowledge, and understanding. The Wisdom God encompassed much more than knowledge. Sagacity about life, common sense, a way of thinking, the search for meaning—all of these were part of the ancient concept of wisdom. In the broadest sense it was both an approach to reality and reality itself.

The idea of the library bears a striking resemblance to this ancient concept of wisdom, incorporating both the process of seeking truth and the truths pursued. What one learned in kindergarten, the seven essential principles, twelve steps to reclaiming your life: the library records all that was thought to be wise—and foolish—yesterday, today, and tomorrow. As the literature on biblical wisdom puts it so succinctly, there is truly nothing new under the sun. And the sum total of all that has come before, including the process of its pursuit, can be imagined existing in the library. Any knowledge that was worthy of being committed to paper can be captured and cataloged in the library, making the institution a most likely candidate for a modern-day version of Sophia, the goddess of wisdom.

"Flashlight" God

Religion scholar Alan Wolfe dubbed the divine presence that gently guides people toward their individual salvation the "flashlight" sense of God. According to Wolfe, this notion of God is most prevalent in America today. Harvey Cox called this aspect of God the merciful, benevolent side that helps people find their way—as he put it, the "oh-so-nice or the user-friendly God." No matter what it is called, libraries—especially reference service—figure perfectly into this image of God. Illuminating, guiding, and helping people find their way.[37]

I, like so many library users, turn to the library as the source of advice and counsel for every question, the solution to every problem. Literally from cradle to grave, I consult the library at every stage of life. How to prepare for pregnancy, toilet train my daughter, plan for retirement, cope with my father's death. Whatever stage of life I am in, the library provides me guidance. Where previous generations sought enlightenment from their religion or holy books, I seek out the library.

God's Still, Small Voice

Beyond being the source of information, the library also provides the place to seek and find those answers that lie deep within one's soul. As described in the Bible, God is not in the wind, or the earthquake, or the fire. Rather, God is found in the still, small voice. But one needs peace and quiet to be able to hear that voice. The library provides one of those few silent spaces where people can be guided to find their answers, whether that source be printed on paper or imprinted on one's heart. Once true silence and contemplation are possible, the inner source of God can emerge.

God the Force

"Whenever I was free to read, the great library seemed free to receive me," said author Alfred Kazin about the New York Public Library. This image of the Great Library accepting and nourishing exemplifies the notion of God the Force. Libraries pulsate with intellectual energy. Germaine Greer—who also imagined libraries as heaven—recognized the power that resides in libraries. "My dream," she said, "was to live in this heavenly building and know all its secrets."[38]

Alan Cohen, vice president of the wireless technology company Airespace (a name with its own religious imagery), referred to the Internet as divine. God, like Google, "is wireless, is everywhere, sees everything." Both can answer any questions in the world.[39] Librarians hearing such a reference to a Google-type God will surely find the description familiar. More than Google, libraries encompass this kind of God. Libraries have been wireless before there were even such things as wires. Libraries are everywhere, all-seeing and all-knowing. Long before Google or the Web even existed, all that was known was held there.

God the Force can be equated to Ranganathan's law of the library as a growing organism. Knowledge is not inert, simply the accumulation of books on shelves. Instead, like a force among us, this imagined living source of energy can be tapped for strength, courage, and power.

God as Something beyond Yourself

The two words most often input into Google are "sex" and "God." Beyond the fact that millions of people are searching for both, God and sex share other similarities. Through both, individuals can escape their isolation, at least temporarily, by communing with Something beyond their isolated self. As we see in chapter 7, reading also melds a person into Something.

Library use is often described as a feeling of loosing oneself, but it is a paradoxically pleasant feeling of disorientation. Being lost is usually a frightening experience, but the loss of self that happens in libraries is oddly comforting. Indescribably, the feeling is often accompanied by an ineffable joining with Something beyond one's self, eliciting a feeling of safety that buffets the loss of self. Within the confines of the library, we can give ourselves up to this greater being, trusting that we will emerge changed, more complete, and somehow uplifted. One other experience approximates this disquieting yet quieting feeling: praying in a house of worship.

God as Communal Memory

Libraries one-up the Google type of God by providing an intimate, sacred experience. Computer-based information is dispensed like a vending machine. You put in one word and get others out. But library usage is rarely such a cold machine-type transaction; rather, it is a process. Much like participation in a religious tradition, the user is immersed in the stream of civilization's written record—the past, present, and future—simultaneously becoming part of it yet remaining separate.

Liberating God

Unlike the gentle, guiding notions of God discussed above, others throughout history have pictured God as the powerful Yahweh "who thundered from the mountaintop."[40] For philosopher Rudolph Otto, this form of God and the accompanying experience of the sacred awaken both a trembling shudder and a sense of fascination. Beyond simply inspiring fear, however, this God carries the power to rectify injustice and embolden the powerless. Both individuals and societies can be liberated through this God, breaking away either from the tyranny of one's own making or from societal injustice.

Though libraries are usually associated with a kinder, gentler sense, they have also empowered people to triumph over nearly hopeless circumstances.

Where previous generations saw God's mighty hand and outstretched arm bringing deliverance, the library can likewise be seen as a triumphant, empowering force. The metaphor of freeing oneself from prison is sometimes used to describe the power of gaining knowledge in the library. Libraries have also been imagined violently. A monk in 1170 saw mightiness in the power of libraries and books. "A monastery without a book chest is like a castle without an armory."[41]

Healing God

When sickness falls, many turn to God for healing or the strength to deal with illness. When this need is combined with the need for medical information, the library becomes a natural source for many people. As public librarians can attest, many patrons come directly to the library from their doctors' offices. Clutching slips of paper on which they have jotted down unintelligible yet frightening medical terms, they seek information and solace about their conditions. Others come with prescriptions for medication they dare not ingest until they have researched the drug and its side effects. Beyond this medical information, others come to the library seeking emotional support to deal with the illness. Where believers of old would consult a priest for a prayer, today many consult a librarian for help locating information, which is often followed by a need for comfort, guidance, and, alas, sometimes prayer as well.

LIBRARY PRAYER

The purpose of the review above is not simply to identify each kind of God but rather to show how library users interact with each—or, to put it in religious terms, how they pray. Prayer is defined as the universal attempt to communicate with the divine. Library users participate in such holy conversations in myriad ways.

Indeed, being a librarian, academic, or lifelong student could be seen as constant communication with a library-like deity. When God is thought of as knowledge itself—all of the wonderful and terrible things people now and always have known—librarians commune with this kind of deity daily.

When God is imagined as a connection to history, every person perusing the "E" section of an academic library or 910 section of their public library could be seen as praying. But so are those checking out *Catcher in the Rye* or the *Fannie Farmer Cookbook*. When the idea of connection to history is expanded to include all written communication, everyone reading in a library can be envisioned praying.

But limiting praying to reading may be too narrow. Watching a movie or listening to a song can also be imagined as connecting to what has gone before. Is a baby boomer listening to the Beatles' *Abbey Road* or an old woman checking out a copy of the movie *Singing in the Rain* not praying? If prayer is connection to the past, that form of sacred communication is exactly what one does in a library.

Others may be praying by simply coming to the library, for just being there may infuse them with the Force. Energy, vibrations, spirit, and life force point to this indescribable essence that seems palpable, especially when standing in one of the great reading rooms of a historic library building. Simply standing quietly amid the grandeur can be an act of devotion. As an awed second grader said upon entering such a massive library reading room, "God lives here."

And who could argue that an alcoholic surreptitiously consulting a book on the twelve-step program, or a pudgy patron perusing the South Beach diet, is not praying? In exercising their zeal for self-improvement, they are seeking divine light for both information and inspiration to change their lives for the better. Karl Marx was surely praying to the liberating God as he read each day in the public library. Malcolm X prayed in the prison library where he found his true liberation. Arguably every social justice movement can trace its beginning to someone reading in a library.

To see how library usage can be likened to prayer, consider the following description of a woman observing the moment of silent prayer during a worship service:

> The whispering stopped. The children were still. Suddenly, she could see inside them, to the quiet, hidden parts where they prayed. She could hear past the top layer of words being said, down to the silent, private wishes that were whispered or barely said at all. She heard the inner longings that accompanied the prescribed words. The air in the sanctuary was teeming with these wishes. The words had become real, and they were streaming out of their bodies.[42]

Though that scene describes a religious service, it could just as well be in a library. As much as houses of worship, people pray in libraries. To see how librarians help, heal, and guide people in their prayers, I turn in chapter 2 to the hidden religious aspects of this sacred profession.

NOTES

1. Wiegand, "Critiquing the Curriculum," 61.
2. Schwartz, *Tree of Souls*, 267; Borges as quoted in Griliches, *Library*, 127.
3. Jer 17:1; Mal 3:16; Ez 2:9–10; 3 Enoch. For more on heavenly books, see Schwartz, *Tree of Souls*, 290–1.
4. For a discussion of this experience, see Maxwell, "Nice Jewish Girl."
5. Wolfe, *Transformation*, 183; Mazur and McCarthy, *God in the Details*, 177.
6. For more on religion as a consumer choice, see Schwartz, *Paradox of Choice*.
7. For more on religious trends in America, see Wolfe, *Transformation*.
8. Prothero, *American Jesus*, 296.
9. Wolfe, *Transformation*, 72; Slone, *Theological Incorrectness*, 10.
10. Wolfe, *Transformation*, 90, 199.
11. Schwartz, *Paradox of Choice*, 39.
12. Bellah et al., *Habits of the Heart*, 221.
13. Carroll and Roof, *Bridging Divided Worlds*, 82–83; see also Roof, *Generation of Seekers*.
14. Carroll and Roof, *Bridging Divided Worlds*, 56.
15. Wolfe, *Transformation*, 14 (emphasis added).
16. As quoted in Nathanson, *Over the Rainbow*, 246.
17. Prothero, *American Jesus*, 155; Grant, O'Neil, and Stephens, "Neosecularization," 483.
18. As described in Nathanson, *Over the Rainbow*, 251.
19. For instance, see Goethals, *TV Ritual*; Mazur and McCarthy, *God in the Details*; Ostwalt, *Secular Steeples*; and Pahl, *Shopping Malls*.
20. As discussed in Magdalinski and Chandler, *With God on Their Side*; see also "Hoops and Heaven: Class Takes a Look." Jan. 15, 2004. http://www.centre.edu/web/news/2004/hoops04.html.
21. Gunston, "Play Ball!" 36.
22. Cox, "The Market as God"; Brooks, *On Paradise Drive*, 212.
23. Roof, "Blood in the Barbecue?" 109–22; see also 106–7. Kroc as quoted in Brooks, *On Paradise Drive*, 213.
24. Jindra, "It's about Faith," 165–79; see also Forbes and Mahan, 15.
25. Nathanson, *Over the Rainbow*, 11.
26. McElroy, *American Beliefs*, 227.
27. Brooks, *On Paradise Drive*, 218.
28. As described in Cox, *Common Prayers*, 160.
29. Prothero, *American Jesus*, 104.
30. As quoted in Edmundson, *Why Read?* 124.
31. As quoted in Moyers, *Moyers on America*, 51.
32. Brooks, *On Paradise Drive*, 76.
33. Moyers, *Moyers on America*, 51.
34. Wolfe, *Transformation*, 91; Woocher, *Sacred Survival*, 67, 92.
35. Prothero, *American Jesus*, 47, 64.

36. Porterfield, *Transformation*, 195.
37. Wolfe, *Transformation*, 165; Cox, *Common Prayers*, 27.
38. Kazin as quoted in Battles, *Library*, 201; Greer as quoted in Griliches, *Library*, 63.
39. As quoted in Friedman, *World Is Flat*, 159.
40. Cox, *Common Prayers*, 2.
41. As quoted in Griliches, *Library*, 95.
42. Mirvis, *Outside World*, 188.

CHAPTER TWO

Librarians Perform Sacred Functions

*I*f libraries are imagined as heavenly, it stands to reason that librarianship is likewise a spiritual profession. As proof that this is so, I offer the following job description taken from the *Encyclopedia of Career and Vocational Guidance*:

> Individuals entering this field need to be outgoing and friendly and have a strong desire to help others. They need to be able to get along with people from a wide variety of backgrounds. They need patience, sympathy and open-mindedness to be able to listen to the problems of others, while maintaining a discreet and sincere respect. They must possess a strong feeling . . . of service, which means giving material success a lower priority.[1]

Does this sound like a job description for a reference librarian? I believe it does. But the profession being described is that of a Protestant minister. I took the liberty of omitting the requirement that individuals feel "God is calling them" to service. Secular librarians may not feel called by God, but they may feel called to serve by Something or Someone they cannot describe.

LIBRARIANS IN MINISTERIAL ROLES

I am not the first to equate libraries and librarians with holy work. Charles Curran called librarians high priests in the early 1990s.[2] A book about Indiana's Carnegie libraries is titled *Temples of Knowledge*. Library historian Matthew Battles noted that the proliferation of the book in the nineteenth century transformed the library "from temple to market, from canon to cornucopia."[3] And at the turn of the twentieth century, R. R. Bowker remarked that the library, almost more than the church, had become the people's temple.[4]

Nor is this the first writing to equate librarians and ministers. In 1953 the librarian at the Yale Divinity School, Raymond Morris, wrote "Theological Librarianship as a Ministry." For him, just walking up and down the stacks was a mystical experience. "Theological librarianship is at its best a ministry," he claimed.[5] Morris was addressing work in a religious library, but his theological reference could easily be applied to secular libraries.

Two major social changes since the 1950s have allowed the closer parallel between librarianship and the ministry. First, the secularizing trend discussed in chapter 1 has changed the role of the clergy. Second, secular professions—including librarianship—have assumed functions once exclusively held by religious authorities.

Especially in recent years, the role of clergy in many American denominations has evolved (or devolved) from high priest to religious authority to counselor. In years gone by, clergy were viewed as holy emissaries, possessing what appeared to believers to be a monopoly on divine intercession. Over time they lost this exclusive domain, becoming more earthly religious authorities than heavenly agents. Though they continued to wield power among the faithful, it was unmistakably a diluted mightiness. Now clergy in many denominations are but one of many sources congregants turn to for advice and counsel. Many still turn to their clergy in times of trouble, but they can just as easily take their troubles to a marriage counselor, social worker, psychotherapist, or television talk show host Oprah Winfrey.

A variety of other secular professions have assumed functions once exclusively held by religious authorities. Doctors, nurses, and hospice workers, among others, have supplanted their role as comforters. A myriad of help-dispensing professions—psychiatric social workers, family therapists, marriage counselors, and the like—have sprung up to fill the void. Librarians have also garnered their share of ministerial roles.

History of Library/Clergy Relationship

Before we look at the ministerial functions of librarianship, it may be useful to examine underlying historical explanations of the similarity. Originally librarians were members of religious orders, serving the dual functions of copying and maintaining book collections. Librarians used to be called *scriptores* (scribes). Catalogers at the Vatican today who collect and compile catalogs still carry this title, making the inhabitants of these jobs arguably the possessors of one of the oldest continuing job descriptions.

The *scriptorium* where they worked was known to be a busy, active place, but along with the bustle of the work it still exuded a religious aura. "There you will find all that God has sent down to earth from heaven . . . and all the worldly wisdom that has been known to the world in various ages," proclaimed one description of a book copying scene.[6]

As late as the 1800s, the library profession continued to draw its practitioners from among the religious. The practice had become so common that Justin Winsor, the first American Library Association president, stated that he no longer wanted the profession filled with "clergymen whose only merit was that bronchitis was a demerit to their original calling." Rather, he sought "positive individuals who had entered their calling by choice."[7] It is interesting to note Winsor's wording; after discouraging the religiously affiliated from the field, he encouraged others to enter this secular "calling."

Librarians as Ministers

Many librarians are uncomfortable seeing their work as a divine calling, more often approaching it as a secular activity. And most of the praying librarians engage in at work tends to be for the end of the day. Middle school librarians—the truly sainted among the profession—are known to pray exceptionally hard!

Joking aside, a profound commitment to be of assistance can be found in all librarians. So passionate is the drive, it could even be interpreted as a secular manifestation of a religious sentiment. The desire to be of service has been, and continues to be, a major draw to the profession. According to one study, 95 percent of librarians said the service orientation of the profession motivated them to become librarians.[8] Another study found that the satisfaction derived by serving people is what new librarians thrive on. "Interacting with the public, dealing with appreciative patrons and seeing people smile" were what new librarians found most fulfilling about the profession.[9]

Library historian Christine Pawley claims that, throughout the history of the profession, librarians have been passionate advocates for their institutions, though sometimes their tone borders on being "celebratory," if not "self-congratulatory." Service more than money has in the past and continues to draws librarians to the field. As Pawley puts it, "Ideological and emotional involvement is essential in a service occupation, especially one where the financial rewards are poor."[10]

Librarians render their service in a secular setting, but the same activity performed in a different setting could be considered religious. According to one dictionary definition, ministers give service, care, or aid and contribute to people's comfort or happiness. This beautiful description of ministerial service could perfectly apply to librarians. In his major study of American Christian thought, religion scholar Stephen Prothero highlighted the religious dimension to service. American Christians believe God is served in serving man. After all, as he puts it, "Jesus was the supreme illustration of Godly service."[11]

No one has claimed that librarians are similarly divine (as far I know), but some may see librarians as the secular, human version of service here on earth.

Librarians as Ascetic, Self-Sacrificing Monks

Considering their conjoined history, it should come as no surprise that librarians, just like monks, are often imagined as impoverished and cloistered. The librarian, just like the monastic, is often pictured toiling away over stacks of books, all the while doing it on behalf of the community. Because of the librarian's contemplative, serene nature and duties that require communing with the world of words and ideas, he or she is imagined to know more than most people. Because librarians remain separated from humanity, they have a more direct line to God, working selflessly for the community and God's sake. The high moral standards for librarians are apparent through the requirements originally proposed for the profession: "a college degree (preferably with a background in Latin and French), a high moral character, an intrinsic sense for order and [what else?] a love for books."[12]

Though not richly rewarded in financial terms, librarians have often been pictured as "high-minded" and rich in serenity and peace. To borrow a phrase from columnist David Brooks, for librarians the holy dollar holds no divinity. Of course, as librarians are well aware, the profession has historically been associated with low salaries. One salary survey from 1928 revealed that hod carriers made almost one-third more than librarians ($0.89 versus $0.60 per hour), though catalogers came close by commanding $0.83 per hour salary.

Naturally, plumbers beat them all at $1.29 per hour. In what may be one of the best understatements about the library profession, a 1929 report summarized that "improvement in these conditions has not yet reached a point where librarianship may be said to receive proper recognition and compensation."[13]

Though improvement of salaries remains a priority, money is not the overriding motivation for those entering the profession. One study of seasoned librarians noted that, "surprisingly, for a profession as notoriously underpaid as librarianship, not a single respondent mentioned salary" as a negative feature of the profession. Still, in keeping with the centrality of service discussed above, librarians did express frustration over the lack of funding for library services.[14] Other studies have shown that for new librarians salary continues to be of lesser importance than sharing in an altruistic profession and making a difference in people's lives.

Another contemporary image of the librarian similar to religious hermits—though granted less severe than that of monks—depicts librarians as sexless, strict, and serious. A ponytailed male librarian joked at a conference: "You know the image. The one with the bun, glasses, sensible shoes. Some librarians take exception to it, but personally, I think the image is great. Just look at me," he said, pointing to his ponytail. "It describes me perfectly."[15]

Frequently this image of the librarian is paired with that of the cold, stern, no-nonsense old maid. "I remember the librarian when I was growing up as being so severe, you were afraid to even cough," remembered one elderly patron.

A perfect depiction of the sexless ascetic librarian can be seen in the movie *It's a Wonderful Life*. The main character regretfully imagines that his untimely death destines his wife to becoming a librarian. *Music Man* shows Marian the Librarian as an uptight spinster dedicated exclusively to the moral uplift of the community. Those who attended Catholic schools in a much earlier era may remember nuns who fit the severe, frightening image so familiar to the old-fashioned librarian stereotype.

Since the beginning of the profession, librarians have been depicted as self-sacrificing. Saint Lawrence the Librarian, the Catholic Church's official saint of librarians and archivists, epitomizes the selfless giving of oneself for a grand cause. In 258 BCE, when Roman imperial guards demanded that Lawrence surrender the Church archives, he hid them, refusing to divulge their location. Even after being lashed to an iron grid and dangled over a charcoal fire, he refused to reveal their whereabouts. "I am roasted enough on this side," he is rumored to have said. "Turn me over and eat."[16]

Librarians as Not-So-Sainted

Of course librarianship, like all professions, has had its share of both saints and scoundrels. One reason the first ALA president stressed high standards for new entrants to the profession may have been the less-than-virtuous history of those choosing the career. Though librarians are fond of trumpeting their goodness, vice rather than virtue motivated at least some of those involved in the establishment of libraries.

Many ancient libraries were founded by stealing and copying books. When the Alexandrian library was created, the Ptolomies ordered the confiscation of any books visitors possessed. Though the stated purpose was for making copies for the libraries, sometimes the originals were kept as well. Librarians can take a perverse pride in the fact that one of the stated purposes of collecting the books was to corner the ancient market in intellectual capital. Though less than virtuous, the motivation is an acknowledgment of the power books can convey.

When the Medici family established what has been called the first modern public library in 1444, some believe the "public" access was in essence a "vehicle of publicity." Though it is true the library benefited society, historian Lisa Jardine believes that its establishment added up to a "recognisable programme of self-promotion and public commemoration" for the Medici family name as much as for the public good.[17]

Thomas Bentley, the librarian of Cambridge's Trinity College, lost his job in 1728 because of unauthorized extended trips to the Continent. Despite his claim that his sole motivation was to "study and acquire books"—central activities, he explained, for any librarian to serve his community—he was duly fired. Among the reasons given for the action was that his presence was needed in the library. As was noted in his dismissal, a chief function of a librarian is to be in the library and "watch each library reader, and never let one out of his sight,"[18] unfortunately remaining as central functions for the profession ever since.

Librarians as Respected Priests

Librarians are not usually referred to with the honorific title of Reverend, but they are a revered population nonetheless. A librarian from the northern portion of the country recounted a minor car accident she had in a rural part of the Deep South. When the young man driving the other car looked at her insurance information, he learned of her place of employment and therefore her profession. "I cain't believe I hit a li—brarian," he said in a classic southern accent. "I'm so sorry," he said sincerely. "I had no idea you were a li—brarian. I cain't believe what I just did. Shaking his head, he repeated, "I hit a li—brarian." The southern drawl of that word continued ringing in her ears throughout her trip, as did his deferential tone. "I felt just like a priest or something, the way he acted when he found out what I did."

Both clergy and librarians are imagined to have a direct line to a higher authority. For the religious, the authority may be considered divine, with God bestowing special access, abilities, or knowledge. For the secular, the source more likely derives from the sum total of civilization's written record. As living representations of traditions, librarians inspire reverence because of the long and glorious history of the institution, along with all the accumulated knowledge it represents.

Perhaps it is this reverence that explains why trial attorneys favor librarians on their juries. Not only do they command the respect of their fellow jurors, they also are trusted for their good judgment and intelligence. From the beginning librarians have been among the most educated of the population by virtue of their literacy. The librarian-scribe was often one of the few people in a town who could read and write.[19] So respected was the profession that Jews in ancient times were not allowed to live in a town that did not have a scribe.

The deference due librarians bears similarities to that of funeral directors, another profession that bestows upon its members a community's trust, value, and respect. One funeral director's brochure proclaimed all members of that profession to be philosophers automatically because they "have caught a glimpse of death and the Force . . . responsible for existence."[20] Librarians are also intimately involved in the Force, but for them it is the Force of Knowledge. Librarians, like funeral directors, come in contact with the dead daily. Though they deal with the corpus of the written word rather than the corpse of a person, perhaps the similarity lends respect to both professions.

At a recent college committee meeting, I was reminded of the respect our profession automatically garners. After introducing myself as the assistant library director, one committee member repeatedly addressed me as "Madam Librarian" throughout the meeting. His tone implied both respect and mocking but revealed what I assumed was an underlying deference for members of my profession.

Other librarians have noted that, upon learning of our occupation, some people immediately try to impress us with their literary and intellectual prowess. "I love the library," "I am a big reader," "I use the library all the time" are all frequent rejoinders from those who learn they are in the presence of a librarian, which brings to mind another similarity between libraries and religious institutions. Surveys respondents frequently overreport both church attendance and library use.[21]

Librarians as Receivers of Confessions

Both librarians and clergy must be able to keep secrets. Because people come to the library and to a house of worship to seek help with serious personal problems, both institutions must guarantee a high level of confidentiality and trust. Indeed, it could be argued that the scandal experienced within the Catholic Church over child abuse accusations was virulent not only because of the abhorrent charges but also because of the perceived violation of this trust.

Alfred Kazin noted with appreciation how librarians protected his privacy: "No matter what I posed to a librarian, no one behind the information desk ever asked me why I needed it."[22] The centrality of patron privacy to librarians is evident in the ALA policy on confidentiality and the Library Bill of Rights. Librarians continue to defend the right of patron privacy, as demonstrated recently by the profession's opposition to the U.S. PATRIOT Act.

Librarians as Prophets for Social Justice

The goal of Habitat for Humanity is "to solve the nation's housing problem one house at a time." For librarians this goal could be stated as "to improve the condition of humanity one person at a time." Regardless of their religious persuasion, all librarians share a faith: belief in the power of the written word to uplift humanity. Librarians see their role as helping not just individuals but society at large (see chapter 5). Reference librarians are key to this social salvation, for they are the ones on the front lines helping one person at a time.

Perhaps that explains why throughout history librarians have been likened to other helping, healing professions. "Intellectual physicians," "apostles of culture," and "social workers of the mind" have all been used to underscore the librarian's role in improving, uplifting, and healing both the individual and society. This emphasis on societal improvement is evident in such organizations as the ALA Social Responsibilities Round Table.

Biblical prophets also raised their voices to bring justice and righteousness to their societies. Wielding the authority of God's power, they beseeched members of the community to uplift and improve the living conditions of their day. The power associated with these prophets is not usually seen among librarians, who have historically been pictured as meek and mild. Yet in an interesting twist to the classic image of librarians, recent depictions show librarians as zealous and even violent protectors of good against evil. Batgirl, a librarian by profession, is the classic comic book heroine battling evil and fighting crime with information power. The television show *Buffy the Vampire Slayer* also depicts a librarian fighting injustice and standing on the side of right.

The controversy over the U.S. PATRIOT Act, resulting in librarians being dubbed "hysterical Ruby Ridge–type radicals," has added to this image as defenders of the public good. An Iraqi librarian even became a cultural hero in her country for valiantly rescuing 30,000 books just days before the library was burned in 2003. Two children's books, *The Librarian of Basra* and *Alia's Mission: Saving the Books of Iraq*, recount her triumphant work. As a character in one of these books proclaims, "It's not necessary to see through walls or fly or have any superpowers to be a real-life superhero."[23] Evidently being a librarian and acting on one's professional convictions is heroic enough.

Librarians as Seers and Gurus

On a recent trip to Miami, the Dalai Lama drew a crowd of several thousand, many of whom had come seeking divine guidance. One such seeker shouted from the audience, "What is one's purpose on earth?"

The Dalai Lama lowered his head and silently reflected for several seconds. He slowly raised his head, studied the face of the questioner, waited dramatically, then stated flatly, "I don't know."[24]

Perhaps the Dalai Lama and the questioner should stop by their local library to find their answers. William Cole once said, "The library is the place where I ask questions I can't get answers to." Susan Allen Toth put it, "When I enter a library . . . I still have a reassuring sense that it is going to tell me all I need to know."[25]

According to the Episcopal Book of Common Prayer, God is the one unto whom all hearts are open, all desires known, and from whom no secrets are hid. But Harvey Cox noted that people act as if the stock market, rather than God, knows the deepest secrets and darkest desires of our heart.[26] Just like God and the stock market, librarians must possess—or at least appear to possess—the gift of divination and the ability to see into an individual's soul.

When perplexed, people have been turning to the library as long as there have been libraries. In 1690, politician and diplomat Sir William Temple wrote that people sought out books as guides, searching for a hand "pointing out the straight upon the road," as well as resolving their doubts. Even Henry

VIII consulted the books of his rapidly growing library to seek guidance and justification for his political and personal actions.[27]

As I discuss later in the chapter, many patrons approach the reference librarian with a confession. Because their inability to use the library is a source of embarrassment and shame, their stated desire may not match their actual need. "Where is the fiction section?" may mean "I'm looking for Stephen King's latest novel." "I need something on U.S. history" translates into "My son needs to do a report on the Spanish-American War." The art of the reference interview, as taught in basic library science classes, enables librarians to rephrase the question tactfully and reexamine the patron until the hidden truth is revealed. As library historian Matthew Battles puts it, "Readers read books; librarians read readers."[28]

This process can be challenging when the patron needs a book on economic history, but when the need is for information on impotence, spouse abuse, or personal bankruptcy, skills far beyond those taught in school are required. When dealing with these types of problems librarians, like men and women of the cloth, must "reach down into the soul" of the person standing before them and help.

Ancient high priests had an advantage contemporary librarians and clergy lack. As Harvey Cox put it,

> In days of old, seers entered a trance state and then informed anxious seekers . . . whether this was an auspicious time to begin a journey, get married or start a war. The prophets of Israel repaired to the desert and then returned to announce whether Yahweh was feeling benevolent or wrathful.[29]

Because their apparent source was the divine, priests supposedly had an inside track to God's omniscience. After peering into a person's heart and knowing their deepest secrets and darkest desires, holy seers could tap holy information. But today psychology and intuition are about all librarians have to work with to know what people really need.

Even catalogers who work behind the library scene are expected to possess this ability to see into the soul of others. They must do so only from the printed word in front of them. The Dewey decimal classification rules instruct librarians that if a book can be classified under two subjects, catalogers should "determine the author's purpose" before issuing a call number.

Librarians as Magicians

Magic and religion have had a complex, at times competitive relationship. Magic is the art of producing a desired result through the use of techniques such as incantations to control supernatural forces. Some would argue that this perfectly describes religious rituals as well.

The Bible frequently inveighs against sorcerers, soothsayers, those who cast out spells and work marvels, warning that these are "abhorrent practices" performed by other people and other nations. At the same time, ancient high priests supervised sacrificial offerings and performed acts that surely would have appeared as magic to members of those other nations. Exactly what made one act religious and the other magical is a fascinating topic but beyond the scope of this book.

What is relevant to the library context, however, is the unknown, secret element of both magic and religious practice. Audience members are not privy to all the information possessed by priests or magicians. Words are intoned in secret, hands waved and items manipulated by way of knowledge and techniques not generally shared by all.

In the same way, librarians produce information that can seem magical—and even miraculous—to library users. My cousin remembered seeing a silly television show years ago about a New York socialite forced to live on a farm, but she could not remember the name of the show. It took me approximately five minutes to locate the name of the show for her—*Green Acres.*

"God, I don't know how you do that!" she said with such enthusiasm that I did not know if she meant "God" as in "Gosh" or was thinking of me as divine at that moment.

Other librarians have their own stories of patrons dazzled and amazed by their ability to produce information seemingly out of thin air. To many it can appear "as if sprung from the brow of Zeus," says Matthew Battles.[30] This is especially true now that so much library information is produced from a computer rather than a printed book. Library users approach the librarian, state what they need, and, poof, from the depth of the machine emerges exactly what they seek. After producing five articles in less than a minute for one patron, Library of Congress reference librarian Thomas Mann explained, "We can show people things they don't ask for."[31]

Library historian Arthur Bostwick reminds us that the modern public library was founded on the dual purpose of finding a reader for every book on its shelves and a book for every reader in a community. "In all cases it should bring book and reader together."[32] "There is a book for every person," claims Ranganathan's Five Laws of Librarianship. Implicit in this union of person and book is an understanding that, by applying a bit of library magic, the librarian can bring about a desired result. Perhaps no supernatural forces will be controlled, but every person touched by her magic will gain access to the universe within the walls of a library.

Librarians as Teachers

Just like in Jesus's parable, librarians prefer to teach library users to fish (so to speak) rather than serve up fish on demand. Library literature constantly reminds librarians that their instructional role is central to the profession. Along with giving patrons the answers they seek, they are encouraged to teach users the research process so they can learn to find information on their own.

According to a *New York Times* article on the changing role of library research, many librarians have found that the new reliance on electronic resources makes their role as guides more important than ever.[33] Though librarians originally feared that technology would replace them, they now see themselves needed more than ever because of the difficulty of conducting research electronically. As one pundit put it, information overload is an important new emotional, social, and political problem. "Almost anybody can *add* information. The difficult question is how to *reduce* it."[34]

Library users being overwhelmed by vast library resources is nothing new. In 1868 Ralph Waldo Emerson noticed students fleeing the library, "repelled by the multitude of books which speak to them of their own ignorance."[35]

EXPLAINING LIBRARIAN/CLERGY SIMILARITIES

Personalities

Besides the religion-like functions of the library profession listed above, similarities can also be found in the personalities of clergy and librarians. According to one online career planning tool, the preferred personality types and skills for members of the clergy are nearly identical to those optimum for librarians. The Myers-Briggs Type Indicator, a well-known personality test that categorizes people according to stated preferences in thinking and perceiving, provides an excellent demonstration of similarities between the two.

Generally acknowledged as the most popular self-insight psychological test in use today, at least a million people take Myers-Briggs every year.[36] By assigning people to one of sixteen different categories, and combining four subscale ratings for each, people can be categorized according to their supposed personality traits. As the chart on this page reveals, librarians and clergy have remarkably similar test results.

Clergy	Librarians
INFJ	INFJ
INTJ	INTJ
ENFP	INFP

(Traits represented by abbreviations:
E = Extraversion; I = Introversion;
S = Sensing; N = Intuition;
T = Thinking; F = Feeling;
J = Judging; P = Perceiving)

Similarly, the online career planning tool Bridges Choices Planner helps students compare their skills to those needed in various occupations.[37] By ranking basic skills such as mathematics and reading comprehension from 1 to 5 (with 1 being the lowest and 5 the highest), individuals can easily plot their own abilities with different careers. As with the Myers-Briggs instrument, the planner on this page shows many similarities between the required abilities for clergy and librarians.

Basic Skill	Clergy	Librarians
Reading comprehension	level 5	level 5
Active listening	level 5	level 4
Writing	level 5	level 4
Speaking	level 5	level 4
Critical thinking	level 4	level 3
Active learning	level 4	level 4
Mathematics	level 1	level 1
Science	level 1	level 1

In his 1950 classic *The Lonely Crowd*, sociologist David Riesman identified three major personality types, which religion professor Stephen Prothero summarized as "tradition-directed people who follow rules written by ancestors; inner-directed people who follow rules laid down by their parents; and other-directed people willing to bend the rules in order to win the approval of their peers."[38] One would assume that both religiously inclined individuals and librarians would qualify for the first personality grouping. Religion by its very nature includes dictates for living that have been inherited from ancestors. Librarians not only serve as the recipients of past traditions but are governed by cataloging and classification rules that accompany them.

Though it is difficult to pinpoint personality traits common among librarians, similar characteristics can be identified among well-known librarians of the past. According to library historian Dee Garrison, Melvil Dewey, the father of modern library science, exhibited "the classic obsessive compulsive personality: order, perfectionism, detail, intellectualization and commitment to work."[39] Many librarians will squirm reading these symptoms, for many of these negative-sounding traits are helpful, and even required, to perform certain functions of the profession. In summarizing the life of the first librarian of the Library of the British Museum, library historian Matthew Battles claims that Antonio Panizzi's progressive ideology and esoteric knowledge prefigured him for a career as a librarian.[40] Panizzi was also a devotee of secret societies, liberal politics, and mysticism, but whether these are librarian predilections is open to debate.

Hypothesizing about librarian traits from history may be a shaky way to unearth the personality characteristics of the profession. One can, however, assume that most librarians today are readers. A survey by the National Endowment for the Arts sheds light on this population group:

> People who read for pleasure [and one would assume librarians figure largely among this group] are many times more likely than those who don't to visit museums and attend musical performances, almost three times as likely to perform volunteer and charity work, and almost twice as likely to attend sporting events. Readers, in other words, are active, while nonreaders—more than half the population—have settled into apathy.[41]

In a photo essay of libraries, Diane Asseo Griliches claimed, "People who love books and want the public to love books must be good people. There are unsung heroes in every field, and I now sing out to those generous, lively and unusual librarians."[42]

Backgrounds and Demographics

Along with certain personality traits, demographic factors may explain the librarian/clergy similarity. The preponderance of women among the profession has been much discussed and need not be rehashed here. Still, it is interesting to note that, like libraries, organized religion is and has been heavily women-dominated. As early as 1691, Cotton Mather complained that "there are far more godly women in the world than there are godly men." One study of American religious history found that in "virtually every religious group in every era in U.S. history, women have outnumbered men."[43]

Since Melvil Dewey's original call for women in the profession, librarianship has been dominated by the "fairer sex." In an oft-quoted lecture on the qualifications of librarians, Dewey said librarians should possess such virtues as "a clear head and a good heart. When I look into the future, I am inclined to think that most men who will achieve this greatness will be women."[44]

Female dominance was not a given in the early years of U.S. librarianship, especially because of concerns about women's potential "questionable health." "The inability of many 'woman assistants' to do the year's work without breaking down, even when a month's vacation is allowed, brings up the question of the employment of women in libraries," reported a 1929 survey of the American Public Library. Potential concerns were, however, allayed by the medical officer of the New York Public Library, who found that woman assistants were in better physical condition than the men.[45]

Another population group that seems to be overrepresented among librarians is the "religiously related," though I am the first to admit that my experience working in a religion-affiliated library may have skewed my observation. But even in my various secular work settings, such as public libraries and publicly funded college libraries, I found many librarians who were former clergy, nuns, or others who had considered joining the clergy sometime in their lives. Likewise, the number of librarians in these settings who were spouses or children of clergy appeared to far exceed that found in other professions, though, again, I stress that this is simply conjecture. Eager library science students should take note: I believe this subject is ripe for research.

There also seems to be a preponderance of librarians deeply fascinated by the topic of religion. Though of course people from all walks of life could be called "religious" and show an interest in the subject, in my experience librarians are especially attracted to religious study.

No studies I know of provide the religious breakdown of the profession, though the racial/ethnic demographics of American librarians is well documented (7.8 percent African American, 5.1 percent Hispanic, as of 2002).[46] Because of the tradition of separation of church and state, statistics on religious affiliations are not routinely asked by the government and tend to be avoided by professional associations. When I tried combining statistics from the ALA and the National Jewish Population Survey (2000–01), it revealed a guesstimate that 16 percent of U.S. professional librarians are Jewish, though they constitute less than 3 percent of the country's population.[47] Additional statistical analysis is needed to verify this estimate and determine the percentages of other religious traditions within the field.

Religious Influence on Librarians

Without surveying librarians for their religious affiliations, it is difficult to surmise what, if any, influence religion has had on librarians throughout history. It is true that the very first issue of the *American Library Journal* reported the journal's founders to have "an *intense faith* in the future of libraries."[48] Tidbits from history reveal that religion played a large part in the lives of many of these individuals. Harvard College, which "began its life as library," was founded by Puritan minister John Harvard. Reflecting his theological interest, three-quarters of the books were on theology, and the library remained a theological library for at least a century. John Cotton Dana, who led a successful attempt to democratize the electoral machinery of the ALA, was a "religious radical."[49] Ranganathan's classification scheme emerged from his background in mathematics and belief in Hindu mysticism, both of which led him to attempt to connect separate pieces in a systematic way.[50]

Religious influences can be seen in Melvil Dewey, who came upon the idea for his famous classification system while in church and referred to the education of librarians as "the suburbs of the holy field." The Victorian demand of duty to God and work, along with a sense of right and duty to authority, was a forceful part of his upbringing. A near-death experience early in life led to what later became an evangelical call for time-saving efficiency and a devotion to the cause of simplified spelling. Dewey was such a crusader against drink and tobacco that a friend remarked, "It is not enough for you to do your duty, but you must make others, as far as possible, see your duty in the same light."[51]

Judith Krug, director of ALA's Office for Intellectual Freedom, partially attributes her tireless efforts in the field of intellectual freedom to her Jewish roots. Though she did not consciously choose her field of interest because she was Jewish, "the values I hold dear made me ideal for this job." And from whence did she develop these values? "From my mother—a Jewish mother, of course—and from my Jewish background, which made it a perfect fit."[52]

Another well-known librarian influenced by the Jewish religion was Golda Meir, who worked at the Milwaukee Public Library before becoming prime minister of Israel. The influence her earlier profession had on her political success can only be guessed at.

Religion-Like Librarianship Values

Similarities can be found not only in the personalities of librarians and members of the clergy but in the values that undergird both professions. A case could be made that librarians subscribe to the basic tenets of liberal Protestantism, whether they are adherents of this faith or not. Librarians will recognize the following underlying beliefs of this faith, summarized by Stephen Prothero.[53] For comparison, these basic tenets are juxtaposed with Ranganathan's Five Laws of Librarianship:

Liberal Protestantism	*Ranganathan's Five Laws*
The goodness of humanity	Every reader his book
Inevitability of progress	Books are for use
	Save the time of the user
Necessity of good works	Every book its reader
Immanence of God in nature, culture, and the human heart	Library is a growing organism

In much of this book I discuss how each of these values is supported and enhanced by library usage. It can be noted briefly here that librarians embrace a belief in human goodness every time they strive to connect a person with a book. Likewise, progress is implied, either through personal self-improvement or societal uplift, through reading. Belief in the necessity of good works is evident in librarians' mission to service. Finally, viewing the library as a growing organism—perhaps not as God but as a living force that will continue in the future as it has in the past—can be seen as a expression of the immanence of the divine.

NOTES

1. Morkes, *Encyclopedia*, 349.
2. Curran, "Two Models," 254.
3. Battles, *Library*, 119.
4. As described in Sapp, *Brief History*, xv.
5. Morris, "Theological Librarianship."
6. As quoted in Tolzmann et al., *Memory of Mankind*, 30.
7. As quoted in Sapp, *Brief History*, xii.
8. Houdyshell, Robles, and Hua, "What Were You Thinking."
9. Newhouse and Spisak, "Fixing the First Job," 45.
10. Pawley, "Reading Apostles of Culture," xix.
11. Prothero, *American Jesus*, 84.
12. Sapp, *Brief History*, xii.
13. Bostwick, *American Public Library*, 232.
14. Jacobsen, "Class of 1988."
15. Besser, "Future of Academic Libraries."
16. As quoted in Hunter, *Developing and Maintaining*, 10.
17. As quoted in Battles, *Library*, 68–69.
18. Ibid., 115–16.
19. Cahill, *How the Irish*, 62.
20. Laderman, *Rest in Peace*, 75.
21. For more on overreporting, see Putnam, *Bowling Alone*, 71.
22. As quoted in Battles, *Library*, 202.
23. As quoted in Lipson, "Iraqi Librarian," B3.
24. Benn, "Dalai Lama in Davie."
25. As quoted in Griliches, *Library*, 49, 97.
26. Cox, "Market as God."
27. Battles, *Library*, 89, 93.
28. Ibid., 148.
29. Cox, "Market as God," 20.
30. Battles, *Library*, 132.
31. As quoted in Hafner, "Old Search Engine."

32. Bostwick, *American Public Library*, 1.
33. Hafner, "Old Search Engine."
34. As quoted in McCabe, *Civic Librarianship*, 100.
35. As quoted in Battles, *Library*, 145.
36. Moore, "Myers-Briggs Type Indicator," 444.
37. The Bridges Choices Planner is available through www.Facts.Org. http://cp .bridges.com/choices/work/compare/Find.do.
38. Prothero, *American Jesus*, 294.
39. Garrison, *Apostles of Culture*, 107.
40. Battles, *Library*, 128.
41. Solomon, "Closing of the American Book."
42. Griliches, *Library*, viii.
43. As quoted in Prothero, *American Jesus*, 56.
44. As quoted in Sapp, *Brief History*, xii.
45. Bostwick, *American Public Library*, 230.
46. U. S. Census Bureau, "Employed Civilians by Occupation," 399.
47. American Library Association, "Number Employed in Libraries"; *National Jewish Population Survey 2000–1*.
48. As quoted in Sapp, *Brief History*, xi (emphasis added).
49. Pawley, "Reading Apostles of Culture."
50. Steckel, "Ranganathan for IA's."
51. As quoted in Garrison, *Apostles of Culture*, 110; see also 108, 117, and Battles, *Library*, 138–40.
52. Judith Krug, personal communication, November 26, 2003.
53. Prothero, *American Jesus*, 79.

CHAPTER THREE

Librarians and Libraries Organize Chaos

*P*ublic speaking is feared by more people than death. Comedian Jerry Seinfeld quips, "That means that at a funeral, people would rather be *in* the coffin than delivering the eulogy." But there is another fear people dread even more than speechmaking, snakes, spiders, and heights combined. Above all, people fear chaos.

"People want order to be able to control their lives," observes David Brooks. Especially when we are surrounded with so much material wealth, stuff can suffocate us. According to market research, the three most important amenities desired by home buyers are extra counter space in the kitchen, storage space in the basement, and plenty of closets, all features that help organize the possessions of everyday living—or at least that give the appearance of an organized life. In a critique of American consumption patterns, Brooks noted how products allow people to spin tales about themselves. By purchasing a Sears utility closet, one imagines attaining that elusive fantasy of an organized and therefore orderly and peaceful life.[1] Home builders feed the fantasy by providing places to put the Cuisinart, the winter sweaters, the extra rolls of toilet paper.

But organizing possessions is just part of the human need to control chaos. Especially in the electronic era, people drown in the sea of information, unable to drop anchor on any solid ground. The deluge of information ironically results in no information. As I noted in an article about the drawbacks of library technology, "It was better to have four books on genealogy than 1,736,388 hits on Google." With so much information available, the sea of bits and bytes engulfs you.[2]

It is revealing that, along with the "information highway" metaphor, surfing the ocean is often used to characterize the limitless Internet. The ocean can seem an uncontrollable force—the ultimate expression of disorder. Water and chaos were prominent features in ancient myths. Evidence of creation and deluge myths have been found inscribed on Sumerian cuneiform tablets of 2600 BCE. In polytheistic religions, ocean gods were imagined as all-powerful behemoths reigning over the seas. Lake gods, on the other hand, were rarely imagined. Indeed, lakes often seem peaceful and calming because their boundaries are visible. Limited and controlled by the shore, there is no need to imagine a comforting presence for a lake. And so it can be for knowledge and existence.

TAMING CHAOS BY NAMING AND ORGANIZING

In many religions God is and has the power to make something out of nothing and nothing out of something. God accomplishes this divine creation through the twin activities of naming and organizing. God, as divine omnipotence, is and has the capacity to define what is real. God can create the boundaries to calm and control chaos, thereby turning an ocean into a lake.

The Hebrew bible, which forms the basis of Judaism, Christianity, and Islam, begins with God creating and bringing order out of chaos. By classifying and (with human help) naming, existence comes into being—first separating light from darkness, day from night, water from sky and dry land. Even man gets separated from woman.

When a couple learns they are going to have a baby, they immediately begin the enjoyable tasks of selecting a name and determining (or guessing at) the sex of the baby. Both activities help create the child in the mind of the parents as it forms in the body of the mother. Mentally giving their offspring a name and placing that individual in the category of either male or female are the first steps to arranging them in the universe of humanity.

According to anthropologist Mary Douglas, all ethnic groups create and enforce social boundaries by separating, dividing, and classifying. The culprit leading people to categorize is not necessarily animosity toward others. Rather, a sense of order results through the religious stories, rituals, traditions, and myths people tell to distinguish themselves from other people.

Americans excel at organizing. Many believe our ability to organize to "get the job done" characterizes the national personality. Senator Albert Beveridge once claimed that "God made Americans the master organizers of the world to establish systems where chaos reigned."[3] Senator Beveridge was careful to keep God as the legitimizer of systems design. Though Americans do it, God ordains it. Picturing a God involved in order making seems natural and easy to see within a library context. Other metaphors for the divine, such as God the Force, God the Healer, God the Liberator, can also be pictured and applied to libraries. But of all these images, God as Knowledge is the easiest to apply to libraries.

LIBRARY AS ORGANIZED WISDOM

In ancient biblical tradition, God was depicted as wisdom. According to Proverbs, wisdom was the first of God's creations and "was there when He set the heavens into place and when He fixed the foundations of the earth" (Prv 8: 27–29). Like the Greek goddess Sophia, wisdom was likened to a woman walking among the people, bringing enlightenment to those open to receiving her insights. Wisdom was frequently referred to not merely in the modern sense of information but rather as a way of thinking, the search for meaning and order, the path to right living. Wisdom could be found in texts, but it was also found in people, sages, nature, folktales, and experience. It is easy to imagine such a divine being as—or at least living in—the library.

In an imaginative rethinking of how people think of God, Harvey Cox describes how the concept of the stock market—which he refers as The Market—has been attributed to comprehensive wisdom. The Market, like God, is able to determine human needs. Humans can tap divine revelation by learning to read when The Market (like God) is apprehensive, relieved, nervous, or jubilant.[4]

Much like Cox's reimagining of God as the stock market, one could substitute The Library for The Market. Though no one library could claim to contain all human knowledge, at least until the advent of the Internet libraries were the only place one could find the accumulated wisdom of mankind. Indeed, one could construct a syllogism:

God is all wisdom.

All wisdom is the accumulated knowledge of the library.

Therefore, God is the accumulated knowledge of the library.

If God is wisdom, the library has surely been his exclusive domicile throughout history. As early as the year 800 CE, the library was described as the place where you find all that God has sent down to earth from heaven, containing all the worldly wisdom that has been made known to the world in various ages.[5] When he is in the stacks of a library, says library historian Matthew Battles, "I have the impression that its volumes contain the entirety of human experience. That they make not a model for, but a model of the universe."[6]

But the library is more than simply the warehouse of wisdom—it is the organized, systematic world of knowledge. Since the beginning of the written word libraries have not only collected knowledge but structured and therefore controlled access to it. One frequent symbol of this imagined organized universe was, and continues to be, the tree. Among the various religious symbols and metaphors representing the chaotic universe at peace—a rainbow, a sunset, a ray of light shining through clouds—the tree represents the orderly, organized, knowable universe.

With branches outstretched, the tree shows how life stretches upward while remaining grounded. With its height, the tree conveys an overarching hierarchy. Like a rainbow it joins sky and earth, but it continues to develop and grow without losing its shape. The tree conveys a continuing dialectic of one piece forming from what exists below—knowledge and the universe unfolding in an orderly, systematic fashion. Unlike the overwhelming, limitless ocean of information, the tree of knowledge is finite and easily grasped. Even children can climb a tree, exploring from branch to branch, slowly ascending at their own speed rather than being engulfed and drowning.

CATALOGING AND CLASSIFYING

Librarians are intimately familiar with the tree as a metaphor for controlling the chaos of the world of information. But the library tree is not imagined as a maple or oak; rather, the tree of library knowledge is the standardized classification system. No matter which system is used—the Dewey decimal classification, Library of Congress, or National Library of Medicine system—all libraries employ a treelike system to control the chaos of knowledge.

Those learning cataloging according to the Dewey decimal classification system are taught the essence of this simple but profound plan. "The subject matter and notation are hierarchical, so that what is true of a given whole is true of all its parts," explains the preface to the abridged Dewey classification system. A book classifier preparing to use the decimal schedule must understand the principle of hierarchy: each entry is a part of and governed by every entry superior to it. "To understand the full meaning and force of 621.3888, [the classifier] must view it as a part of 621.388, which in turn is a part of 621.38, which is a part of 621.3, which is a part of 621, which is a part of 620, which is a part of 600."[7]

Catalogers take those "miserable things"—square pegs of knowledge that don't fit anywhere—and place them carefully into a grand, organized scheme.[8] Without this placement and structure, the knowledge being classified would never be found, its existence obliterated. Bookstores are good examples of generalized groupings of information that lack the tender touch of the cataloger. A study that compared bookstore and library arrangements concluded that "libraries are systemically superior to bookstores." Though many requests for information can be found in bookstores, libraries do a better job of leading to specific information needs. Especially effective, noted the study, was the fact that libraries "are arranged to allow patrons to locate information effectively and to utilize that information from one library to the next."[9]

One of the best ways to see the importance of the classification and cataloging functions of libraries is to look at the Internet, where these functions are by and large missing. Frustration runs rampant when searching the Web for specific information. Indeed, many people come to the library after hours of fruitless computer searching on their own. I remember a student asking me for information on an obscure American poet. As I headed to the closest computer, she grabbed my arm and physically restrained me. "No," she insisted. "I have already used the computer at home and couldn't find anything. I need something besides that." The information I located for her—which she gratefully acknowledged as exactly what she needed—was obtained through the computer. I had, however, been able to locate and retrieve it thanks to the organized system of periodical databases created by librarians.

Few realize the power librarians wield when they categorize and classify information. As mentioned at the beginning of this chapter, mothers and fathers, gods and God create by naming and organizing. Librarians do so as well when they order knowledge. Rather than fashion their world with clay or earth, librarian-gods breathe life into existence by providing structure. A world of random objects without context is nothing more than uncontrolled chaos. But librarians create connections by naming knowledge and placing it within an organized scheme. Becoming intellectual demiurges, librarians act as supernatural beings, creating and fashioning the world of knowledge as they please.

Librarians' vital but frequently unacknowledged systematic approach to knowledge was brought home to me when my husband's picture appeared in a regional health magazine. Having benefited from a new surgical procedure, he literally became its poster child when the magazine included his picture in an article about the benefits of the operation. A friend noticed his photo, cut it out, and sent it to me. She did so, however, without noting any bibliographic information about the source of the magazine. No librarian would have sent such a photo without at least some bibliographic reference. With our intrinsic sense of order, librarians know that in the future this unidentified photo will be like an isolated tidbit. Without any context to the person or source, in no time this picture will be unidentifiable and useless. It will be as if it never existed.

What makes the librarian's power even more awesome is the comprehensive nature of the organized system libraries have created. Thanks to the voluntary standardization librarians have assumed for their craft, a higher authority legitimizes their pronouncements. National, even global submission is demanded to their proclamations of placement within this comprehensive system. "Class here," "Class elsewhere," "See," or "See also," declares the voice from on high, directing their actions as they place every bit of knowledge in its place within the universe. The actions—and thinking processes—of millions of library users forever are affected by their work.

Like gods, catalogers look into people's hearts. If a book has two subjects, they must determine the author's purpose. A Phoenix schedule gives librarians the power to destroy by retiring subject headings no longer needed. Librarians can mercilessly obliterate entire bodies of knowledge from the face of the earth and from civilization entirely.

HISTORICAL ROLE OF LIBRARIANS AS KNOWLEDGE ORGANIZERS

Librarians have been representing the universe of knowledge through organized systems for thousands of years. As Matthew Battles reports in his excellent library history, as far back as the seventh century BCE the 25,000-tablet library in the city of Nineveh was highly organized. In this ancient library, the tablets were tied together, marked with a label, and cataloged with the titles of works and the number of tablets in the group. The famous Alexandrian library was also systematically organized, with scroll tags including author and title information. Because the scrolls would not stand up on shelves (a later innovation that came with codices), they were heaped together into precarious piles. When one scroll was removed, the others would all need to be shifted, so only a kind of generalized order was possible.[10]

Eventually cards were employed to help locate physical items. Because the original cards were playing cards, the contents of those much-beloved card catalogs approximated the size and shape of a deck of cards.[11]

Before the days of Melvil Dewey, the order of library books was primarily location-based, with books shelved by accession number. As late as 1929, one survey of U.S. libraries found that arranging books on the shelves in the order received was still in vogue, especially in small libraries.[12] The card catalog provided numerical information about the book's location. The innovation for which Dewey is most often credited is arranging books both by location and subject. He "married two systems—one epistemological and one numerical."[13] The numbers in his system were not just designations of a shelving system; they also showed the relationships among the fields of knowledge. This idea, which Dewey claims came to him while sitting in church, was to place all human knowledge into "ten tight holes." Within his system, any book's "subject matter and the notation are hierarchical; so that what is true of a given whole is true of all its parts."

Dewey believed that virtually any given set of objects could be classified by placing together objects with certain characteristics in common and separating them from objects without these characteristics. At the very core of this system is the belief that the disorganized, confusing tumult of our world can be tamed and transformed into an orderly, systematic arrangement. When imagined within such a framework, where a book is classified reveals not simply information about its contents but also its place within the hierarchy of all human knowledge.

Implicit in this arrangement is a belief in the rational order of the universe. "The schedules are developed according to logical principles." The logic of the universe is reflected in the logic of the system. Classification of books assumes an idealized overarching structure of knowledge and truth. Catalogers using the Dewey decimal classification system are urged "to make correct decisions" concerning the placement of material with the scheme, assuming there is a right way to classify not only that one book but the world at large. As Battles puts it, one could imagine that rearranging the books on the shelves "would reveal mysteries of the universe, a sacred logos tantamount to the secret name of God."[14]

Whether godly or not, providing order to knowledge remains a vital service. Antonio Panizzi, nineteenth-century librarian at the British Museum and one of the founders of modern cataloging, saw the very future of humankind at stake through the act of cataloging. The library catalog, he claimed, is "more than a list, more even than a guide to knowledge: it could be the means to transform society itself." By providing what he described as easy access to the works of a library collection, the catalog throws open the doors of knowledge. The humble card catalog provided "the poor student the same means of indulging his learned curiosity . . . as the richest man in the kingdom."[15]

ORGANIZING KNOWLEDGE: MISSION IMPOSSIBLE

Lest we get carried away with these notions of librarian organizing power, the limits of this ability must be admitted. First and foremost among the obstacles is the rate of information pouring forth. Knowledge is doubling at the rate of 100 percent every twenty months. "What you know now will be obsolete by Christmas," claims Frank Ogden.[16] Especially with the Internet, the flow of information is overwhelming. The idea that this tidal wave of inundating information (to return to the water metaphor) can be harnessed, captured, and controlled for even a millisecond seems quaint at best. Foolhardy seems a more apt description.

Though librarians have made valiant attempts to treat Internet sites like books—describing and organizing them with controlled vocabulary and structured hierarchies—to date these efforts have met with limited success. Though technological developments may improve such efforts in the future, for the time being it does not appear that librarians will be able to locate, describe, categorize, and arrange the totality of electronic information.

Some have argued that librarians never have been able to control the flow of printed information because the task of organizing knowledge itself is impossible. As anyone who has pursued academic study recently knows, belief in a purely rationalistic, ordered universe with universally applicable rules and standards is distinctly out of fashion. One of the only definite laws governing the postmodern academic world is that there are no definite laws. Belief in an overarching reality—one that purports to be the same for everyone regardless of perspective or personal stance—is no longer accepted on face value. When rationalist thought itself is called into question, belief that any structure can adequately organize knowledge also grows suspect.

If there is nothing absolutely the same for all, how can one organizing principle universally apply? Attempting to organize all of human knowledge into ten categories—or even ten thousand categories—seems a futile, even impossible task. According to this theory, if every person on earth has a legitimate way of viewing and organizing the world, there must be at least that many organizing systems.

Even without calling the process of organizing knowledge into question, it could be argued that libraries never managed the task adequately in the first place. Even the revered Dewey decimal classification system is decided by a committee. After the publication of the fifteenth edition of this national classification standard, the editors solicited criticism so that successive editors could "bring out the perfect book." Despite their optimism, no future editions have claimed perfection.

And perfect or not, many classification systems are simply too complicated for many libraries. Dewey's first decimal classification system, published in 1873, was 42 pages long. By 1894 it had grown to 467 pages but was too complicated for many small libraries. An abridged edition of 194 pages was published that year to remedy the problem, but recurring complaints insisted that even the shortened version had become "too detailed and complex for the small collections for which they were intended." Though most libraries struggle to contain the information on their shelves through some organizational structure, the effort can be daunting. Just like the scrolls heaped into precarious piles, some small and large libraries today manage to maintain "only a kind of generalized order."[17]

Despite these limitations on their ability to organize knowledge, a perception still exists that libraries manage the task well enough. With the "generalized order" they offer, library users can locate the information they are seeking or stumble upon that which they need but did not know existed.

Linda Weltner believed that having access to the library's world wisdom was all she needed in life. "As long as I can read, nothing human is beyond my understanding."[18] Anne Lamott extolled the virtues of stumbling upon unknown treasures. She credits her mother with teaching her how to use a library when she was a child. "If you insist on having a destination when you come into a library, you're shortchanging yourself." Instead, to find small miracles and truth, one must "wander, letting the book take you where it will." Lamott poetically described the pleasures that await one who follows this advice. Finding and reading library books "is like breathing fresh ocean air," or eating homegrown tomatoes. In the space between words, in the margins, she found the "juicy moments of life and spirit and friendship."[19]

NOTES

1. Brooks, *On Paradise Drive*, 210.
2. Maxwell, "Seven Deadly Sins," 42. For more on the chaos of the Internet, see Rosen, *Talmud*.
3. Roberts, *Who We Are Now*, 221.
4. Cox, "Market as God."
5. Tolzmann et al., *Memory of Mankind*, 30, 31.
6. Battles, *Library*, 6.
7. Dewey, *Abridged Classification*, 14.
8. Morris, "Theological Librarianship."
9. Brisco, "Dewey or Dalton?" 36–37.
10. Battles, *Library*, 25, 28.
11. Ibid., 104, 142.
12. Bostwick, *American Public Library*, 181.
13. Battles, *Library*, 139.
14. Ibid., 6.
15. Ibid., 131.
16. As quoted in Sapp, *Brief History*, 203.
17. Battles, *Library*, 28.
18. As quoted in Griliches, *Library*, 51.
19. Lamott, *Plan B*, 142–43.

Librarians and Libraries Bestow Immortality

ibetan monks are required to spend one week sleeping in a cemetery. Christians must put ashes on their foreheads once a year to remind them that they are but dust. Jews annually recite in unison the most horrific list of disasters that could possibly befall them. Religions force these rituals upon their adherents because of the inherent tendency in all of us to forget our mortality. As theologian Harvey Cox noted, by ensconcing themselves into gated communities and purchasing expensive health insurance policies and retirement plans, people fool themselves into thinking they are beyond mortal danger; even so, disaster can strike at any moment.[1]

Often it takes a life-threatening illness or other tragedy to awaken the fragility of life. A woman who worked with cancer survivors came to see the world divided into two kinds of people: those who have been in contact with their own fragility and those who have not. Those who face death squarely in the face never leave the experience unchanged.

Religion is vital in helping people confront their mortality. For some an everlasting heaven triumphing over the finality of life is imagined and embraced. Other religions offer faith, works, and grace as hoped-for avenues to everlasting life. Still others imagine their good deeds on earth and loved ones' memories granting them eternal satisfaction.

Along with these religious paths to immortality, secular pathways also lead to an imagined life beyond life.

CONSTANT CHANGE AND NEED FOR PERMANENCE

As librarians and library users are painfully aware, the rate of technological change is unprecedented. So fast are things changing that in 2003 an international "Accelerating Change Conference" was held to examine, not the changes swirling about us, but only their dizzying pace. One of the frightening questions addressed at the meeting was whether runaway technological advances are outstripping our ability to even comprehend them.[2] The reasons behind this oxymoronic "permanent change" are varied.

Consumerism may be one culprit. Alexis de Tocqueville noted that Americans seemed spiritually adrift in their land of plenty because they did not know how to orient their lives. "Material goods are the sole fixed point, the sole incontestable value amidst the uncertainty of all things." Henry Steele Commager believes the excessive nervous vitality of Americans is the reason for our sense of instability and rootlessness. There is an "air of impermanence to almost everything Americans undertook."[3]

I once observed an example of confusion wrought by constant consumer product impermanence when I overheard an old man muttering to himself in the grocery store cereal aisle: "Darn it, where is it? Where is it?" he repeated as a mantra. After several minutes of frustrated searching, he shouted "Damn it, they don't make Toasted Frosties anymore!" He walloped his cart with a punishing blow, sending it spinning into the Quaker Cream of Wheat cartons. I understood his frustration all too well. The discontinuation of the one-pound can of Maxwell House Colombian Supreme has produced my own incidents of shopping cart assault.

Missing cereals and coffee cans are not the only victims of capitalism's continuing changes. "No manufacturing plan is permanent . . . against competition," claims urbanist W. Rae Douglas. "No system of transportation withstands disruptive change, no corporation is immune to takeover or bankruptcy."[4] Jobs are no longer permanent. Neighbors come and go. With the rate of divorce, even spouses can seem impermanent fixtures in people's lives.

When times are unsettled as they are now, people long to identify with something that will not disappear or change before their very eyes. The constant, frenetic pace of change reminds us that nothing lasts. No product, service, place, or thing is guaranteed to be here in the future. And, of course, neither will we. And so we long to unite with something or some institution that will stay the same, or at least give the appearance of permanence in our very impermanent world.

The problem is that any institution that manages to remain unchanged will become obsolete and be replaced—because institutions, just like people, must adapt to survive. Yet those very adaptations that guarantee an institution's continuation weaken its historical continuity. A precarious balancing act is required for any institution to provide a sense of permanence in this temporary world. Organizations that survive must constantly change to remain relevant, while appearing to be unchanged in the process.

There are two institutions that appear unchanging as they change, that remain current in people's lives while continually blending past, present, and future. Religion is one. Libraries are the other. Standing like a rock of ages, a mighty fortress, both libraries and religions appear to live on without changing, though in truth both experience change continually.

INSTITUTIONS AS LIVING ORGANISMS

For an institution to appear to live on indefinitely, it must appear to be alive. Religious institutions liken their communities to living beings. The Catholic Church refers to the community of the faithful as the Body of Christ, reflecting the ability of the populace to keep on living beyond the life of any one individual member. Jews call themselves Israel in the plural, not referring to the country but rather to the idea of a continuing community.

Libraries, too, have been seen as living institutions. "The library is a growing organism," states Law Five of Ranganathan's basic guideposts for the modern library. Library historian Matthew Battles poetically sees the library breathing, "exhaling at the start of the term and inhaling at the end, when the books fly back."[5]

Perhaps it is this sense of a living, breathing library, alive with some indescribable life force, that draws people to the library. People are attracted to libraries for reasons far more profound than simply needing information (see chapter 6). Many come to immerse themselves in the library's energy. Inspiration—from the Latin term for "to breathe"—seems to occur within the library walls. Simply sitting among the books, one feels immersed in an aura of living spirit.

One reason libraries feel so alive is that each book on the shelf seems animated. Books have often been referred to as living beings, described through references to birth, death, and life everlasting. "A book is as close to a living thing as you could get without being one," said Bill Harley. Books are sometimes imagined as living people transformed into paper. Ralph Waldo Emerson felt surrounded by "many hundreds of dear friends" when in a library. Alfred Kazin said that every time he was in a library, he "wanted to grab up every book, press into every single mind right there on the open shelves."[6]

Writers often refer to the act of writing as giving birth. "The joy of working on a manuscript," claims publisher-turned-agent Betsy Lerner "is not unlike the midwife's joy."[7] At the other end of the life span, unwanted library donations are often called "book graveyards." Jews historically had, and continue to observe, strict regulations governing the disposal of sacred books. A special graveyard for books called the Genizah provides a permanent resting place for books no longer needed. They must be buried because "the contents of books go to heaven like the soul."[8]

But the fact that religious institutions and libraries seem to be alive and contain living beings does not in and of itself grant immortality. To convey a sense of life everlasting effectively, the institution must also provide a way for the individual to feel a part of the collapsed past, present, and future of the institutional thread. Religions and libraries attain this through communal memory, history, and the printed word.

COMMUNAL MEMORY

Shared communal memory is like a river, said Bill Moyers, "dynamic and changing, bearing the heritage of the past to water the fields of the present." The waters of the river feel comforting and refreshing. When one stands in the river of religious heritage, one feels immortally immersed in and surrounded by the past, present, and future.[9] Religious traditions constantly repeat their shared history—their communal memory—to enable the faithful to stand in the past and present simultaneously. By enacting the remembered history through narrative, myth, and ritual, people are encouraged to bring to mind and identify with those who came before them.

The word "remember" is used on 169 occasions in the Bible. Even God is told to remember and can be reprimanded should he fail to do so. Psalm 44 scolds God for not remembering, suggesting that he may have fallen asleep on the job.

For religious communal memory to seem legitimate, it must be steeped in history. The regalia of the clergy, décor of the house of worship, and religious artifacts convey the historical message of the religion. The words repeated in the liturgy, holiday rituals, and communal myths all bring to mind imagined historical moments. Life cycle events frequently evoke the memories of those who came before, bringing a sense of continuity and history to everyday lives.

But remembering is just the first part of the process. The person approaching a tradition does not do so objectively but comes with a desire to join with it, own it—"commune with it," to use the religious term. By doing so, people can vicariously gain a sense of immortality. To believers, this unending tradition seems somehow good, complete, and holy. Enmeshing oneself in a historical tradition seems melding into an aspect of God. The narrative history of a people can take on divine characteristics (see chapter 1). Even if parts of the remembered history are tragic, violent, humiliating, and better left unremembered, participating in the continuing historical experience can feel like a holy experience. The act of remembering may even strengthen the religion itself. "To belong to a tradition is to become part of a chain, and the longer the chain, the more secure each individual link."[10]

Obviously libraries capture and preserve communal memory; indeed, it is their reason for being. As Goethe put it, libraries serve as "the memory of mankind." The library does not require 169 biblical commandments to remember. Preserving the written record of civilization is the purpose of the institution's existence: "Libraries should provide materials and information presenting all points of view on current and historical issues," proclaims Article II of the ALA's Library Bill of Rights. In fulfilling this directive, libraries are preserving the memory of the past and present for generations to come.

In his book on library history, Matthew Battles speaks of a "universal library," imagined as the totality of knowledge gathered, organized, and preserved for all time. Longfellow said libraries contain it all, both "the ruins of an antique world, and the glories of a modern one." The Internet has been referred to as the sea of information. Others may see it as the river of knowledge, evoking the same image Moyers used to describe a religious tradition.

Francis Lieber saw libraries not as the water but as "the bridges over which civilization travels from generation to generation."[11] When imagined this way, the act of checking out a book from a library can be seen as dipping into or crossing over the river of accumulated, historical knowledge. Whether one checks out *The Prince* from the 1500s or *Men Are from Mars, Women Are from*

Venus, library users interact daily with the accumulated record of humankind.

Cognizant of their special role in preserving printed history, librarians have a special reverence for history. I saw a demonstration of this one day when I visited the journalism office at my college, hoping to make a copy of an early issue of the school newspaper. I asked the editor if I could borrow the original—the only known copy—and take it to my office.

"Normally I would say no," he said. "But since you are a librarian, it's okay."

IMMORTALITY THROUGH WORDS AND BOOKS

As the newspaper editor knew, librarians revere the written word. They do so because words pack a powerful punch. "In the beginning was the Word, and the Word was with God, and the Word was God," begins the New Testament's Gospel of John. In traditional Judaism even the name of God cannot be written because of its power; it is shown in print only as an abbreviation. Even in secular language, some words are associated with great power. The word "abracadabra" is the rendered version of a religious incantation, which supposedly created matter with its utterance. Simply saying certain words can bring disaster. "Break a leg" is offered to actors rather than "Good luck" because the latter said aloud will evoke long-sleeping theater spirits.

Especially when committed to paper and gathered together as a book, words become potent. Christian and Jewish worship services ritually incorporate books. In the central part of Jewish service, the Torah (a library itself) is brought from the ark and shared among the people. Catholic worship services include a Bible with other holy religious objects as part of the religious ritual. By incorporating books into their worship, religions demonstrate the central place of their revered written text. Here, they announce to the congregants, is the written story of our people and our faith.

Individuals, too, use books to record and proclaim their own stories and faith. Intellectual historian Warren Susman noted that historians cannot claim for themselves a monopoly on history: "Everyman—and every woman and child—is in some fundamental sense his own historian."[12] This desire to record one's presence on earth leads some to carve their initials on trees, drives others to press their hands into soft sidewalk cement, and inspires some to create or sell books. Books, according to John Milton, are a means to achieving "life beyond life."

A character in a Jonathan Rosen novel contemplated this immortal aspect of books when planning his suicide. After gathering the drugs and scotch that would accomplish the task, "he stood for a moment in front of the vast book-shelf that formed one whole wall of his study. There were many books in several languages. Poetry. Novels. Histories. Prayer books. Somehow, they would have to speak for him. Part of him would live in those books."[13]

According to writer/publisher/agent Betsy Lerner, immortality affects not just authors but others in the book trade:

> Just as the author hopes for immortality through publication of his book, most people in publishing hope to work on a book that touches people, entertains them, enlightens them, or changes them, a book that shapes the national dialogue or becomes a part of the lexicon. Publishing people, along with the author, believe that a book can still be a force of nature.[14]

The desire to conquer immortality drives others to embark on the arduous task of writing a book, acknowledged by authors everywhere as a laborious undertaking. "Writing a book is horrible," said George Orwell,

> an exhausting struggle, like a long bout of some painful illness. One would never undertake such a thing if one were not driven by some demon whom one can neither resist nor understand. For all one knows that demon is simply the same instinct that makes a baby squall for attention.[15]

While in the process of producing a manuscript, philosopher and cultural critic Walter Benjamin claimed the book was more important than he was.

Whether driven by demons or inspired by angels, people continue to write books. Imagining a descendant generations from now discovering one's writing in a dusty attic is a heavenly thought. Likewise, eternal damnation could be defined as seeing one's magnum opus buried under chicken bones in the garbage can. And so we write books.

Bill Moyers reported his delight when asked to write a book. "Few things flatter a broadcast journalist more than the prospect of even the briefest half-life between hard covers," he says. "Like ice, we melt into the milieu. We're lucky if someday a grandchild or a graduate student is curious about what we once said. Writing a book allows you to connect the dots between past and present."[16]

Library Immortality

If writing a book offers an author a "half-life" of perceived immortality, getting that book onto the library shelf seems to extend the period eternally. It is imagined that the words of one's soul, if not one's soul itself, can live forever in a library. Schopenhauer clarified Goethe's characterization of the library as "the *papered* memorial of mankind."[17] Authors clamor to have their words included among these library papers.

Librarians are well aware of the pull of the library shelves. Imagining generations to come reading their words drives authors to dump their manuscripts and self-published books on libraries. Others empty their attics and basements of once-beloved books, offering up these overstuffed Burdine's bags and brimming Tide boxes in the hopes of winning a place on a library shelf. Here on a library bookshelf their words will live on everlasting. The library offers a link with an anonymous public that no attic can match. "Unlike a private book, a library book continues to open doors."[18]

The appeal of the library stacks was demonstrated to me firsthand when, as a college library director, I instituted a formal ceremony called "Barry Authors Reception." Any college faculty, student, or staff who had penned a book during the year would be allowed to ceremoniously present their book to the library. Throughout my thirty-year library career, few other programs or services have been as successful. During the wine and cheese reception that followed, I was thanked repeatedly for initiating this program. As one faculty member put it, "People don't realize what goes into writing a book."

Evidently the creation of the authors program had tapped an unrecognized (and perhaps exploitable) fact that, as Battles put it, "inclusion in the library represents a landmark in a literary life."[19] A study of the history of the Charleston Library Society revealed that local churches had donated books about their religious congregation to the local library, even though the materials were freely available to parishioners through the church. Apparently the presence of these books in the library legitimized their organization.

As described in a short story by Max Beerbohm, one fictionalized author even made a deal with the devil to live eternally in hell in exchange for an opportunity to visit the British Library's reading room one hundred years later to see his books amid the library collection. Ironically, Battles mused in the pages of his book on library history where it would be in the library. "Where will I find the book you are reading now?" Will it be "history, memoir, or fiction?"[20] I must confess to having the same thoughts as I typed this work. It is one thing to have one's book written and published, but the pinnacle of publishing lies in securing the placement of one's words on a library shelf.

Immortal Citations

Having your words placed for perpetuity on the library shelves is only part of the process. For future generations to find one's noble words, access to these writings must be organized, classified, located, and retrieved. In chapter 3 we saw the lofty role librarians play in this process. Here it should be mentioned that citing a source in MLA format, though it may seem devilish work to the nascent student, is actually a heavenly act. When done right, the "Works Cited" page grants immortality to both the writer of the paper and the source cited.

Citations are so important that they have even been credited with creating the Internet as we know it today. The desire to improve the existing academic system of citation led Tim Berners-Lee to create the World Wide Web. The desire to reverse the process led Larry Page and Sergey Brin to create what later became Google. As John Battelle notes in *Wired* magazine, "The needle that threads these efforts together—the practice of pointing to other people's work . . . is the citation."[21]

Citations are critical because, as both religions and librarians acknowledge, great truths can emerge from the written word, but so can dire consequences from misstatements and falsehoods. To protect against this, both religions and libraries employed elaborate systems of quality control. In religions this was attained through rules governing the copying, distribution, public reading, and treatment of holy texts. Libraries relied on the sacred system of citations.

Anthropologists have found that in oral, nonliterate cultures a person's word takes on special meaning. Examples of the importance of the spoken word can be seen in the frequent instances in the Bible of bestowing a blessing or swearing an oath. So important was the latter that men uttered them, not by raising their hand, but by placing it on their genitals, graphically demonstrating that future generations would abide by what was being sworn (Gn 24:2–3).

When literacy spread, the reliance on accuracy remained an important concern. The scribes who copied manuscripts were under strict requirements to duplicate their material accurately. During the Middle Ages Christian monasteries, which were the setting for *scriptoria*, instituted elaborate quality control measures to certify the fidelity of text copies. A *precentor* who also sometimes served as the librarian supervised the copying of texts. The *precentor* would choose and present a text to each scribe. If the scribe refused to copy the selected text, the *precentor* could "deprive him of his wine." After being copied, texts were examined by at least one and sometimes two correctors.[22]

Because accurate copying required extreme concentration, after silent reading became the norm around the ninth century scribes were required to work in silence. When they needed a certain book for reference in their work, they pantomimed hand signals. Placing the hands on the head in the shape of a crown referred to King David and meant "pass the psalter." "I need the missal" was communicated by making the sign of the cross. In those pre–politically correct times, scratching the body like a dog referred to pagan works.[23]

St. Jerome required his scribes to transmit a formula attributed to St. Ireneus that threatened "the Lord Jesus Christ in His glorious Second Coming, will come to . . . compare what you have copied against the original."[24] Sometimes scribes were allowed to sign their work and add a personal expression in the text. "So be it," "Peace," and "Amen" were written. Often the words "Thank goodness it's finished!" were added. Modern-day librarians will be heartened to learn that one scribe ended his manuscript with the complaint that his work was fruitless since nobody reads books today.

Judaism established elaborate rules for the public reading of the Torah to ensure its accurate recitation, with many of these ritually incorporated into the current worship service. In some synagogues on Monday, Thursday, and Saturday when the Torah is read aloud, a *gabbai* must be present to look over the reader's shoulder to guarantee that every syllable is chanted correctly. As nervous bar and bat mitzvah boys and girls know, the *gabbai* is obligated to correct the slightest mispronunciation made by the chanter. When the Torah is lifted from the lectern to be wrapped and returned to the ark, it is mandatory that several columns of text be shown to the public, ensuring that everyone in the congregation can see the text personally.

The Talmud, a massive compilation of biblical commentary, meticulously credits the source of quotations and arguments. A heavenly reward is promised to those who cite accurately. "One who recalls a teaching in the name of its author brings redemption to the world," claims Rabbi Elazar in the name of Rabbi Haninha. Naturally, the quote includes a citation.[25]

Footnotes are the *gabbais* of the academic world, or, as Princeton University historian Anthony Grafton put it, the high whine of the dentist's drill inflicting random but necessary pain. Though students may experience footnotes as a pain in a different part of their anatomy, Grafton says they absolutely matter. "Arguments . . . stride forward or totter backward" solely through these funny little asterisks and elevated numbers.[26]

Writer Mary Gordon knows firsthand the power of citations to bring the dead back to life. As she recounts in the biography of her father, *Shadow Man*, by following citations to his writing, Gordon was able to reconstruct the life of her father, who died when she was seven. As she recounts dramatically, with the help of tireless librarians and the interlibrary loan system she was able to locate the "anti-Semitic articles and pretentious literary journalism" her father wrote. Ultimately her search of archives and libraries revealed the "bombshell truth" that her father was not the Catholic Harvard graduate of family lore but rather a Jewish high school dropout from Vilva, Lithuania.

LIMITS TO LIBRARY IMMORTALITY

Mary Gordon was lucky. She was able to assemble the facts of her father's life because Brown University still had a copy of *Hot Dog: A Monthly for Regular Fellows* in a cardboard box. This archive, along with an elaborate trail of indexes, microfilm, and print resources, enabled her to piece together the story of her father's life.

But as Nicholson Baker made painfully obvious in his scorching book on library print withdrawals, *Double Fold*, fewer and fewer libraries are able to maintain print collections at the levels they once did. Given shrinking libraries and electronic resources, immorality through the library shelves may be more myth than reality. When pressed, most people—and librarians—will acknowledge the cruel fact that even the vast holdings of all the libraries of the world cannot contain and preserve the complete written record of human knowledge. But as with religious practice, we wink about ourselves and continue as if we had not recognized that fact. Librarians are aware of the extensive winking that is needed. Because publishers cannot afford to warehouse low-demand books, they rely on libraries to provide access to these titles. Calvin Trillin quipped that the life of a book is somewhere between that of milk and yogurt.

Libraries are, however, less and less able to fill the need for permanent book conservatories. Administrators with budgetary control over libraries believe, like so many people, that "everything is on the Internet." Therefore, they are reluctant to commit scarce funds to construct buildings to house substantial print collections. Without the promise of more space, librarians must painfully withdraw existing materials in order to make space for the new. Though collection weeding has long been a standard of basic librarianship, the pressure to withdraw, withdraw, withdraw to make room for the new has grown to what in some libraries is crisis level.

What happens to all of those weeded books is always a powder keg problem for librarians. "I sneak out to the dumpster at night," confesses one librarian, "so no one will see me throwing away books." Many librarians resort to this tactic, knowing that the sight of unused, discarded books can inflame the public like little else.

Perhaps the sight of books in trash cans affects the soul because of the imagined end of the immortality of the books' authors. Or maybe the thought of a useful resource going to waste, like the sin of throwing away food, is troubling. Boxes of college textbooks are dragged from apartment to condo to house for no known reason. The same reluctance to toss a book means that librarians must either conceal the fact that they discard books or try to find them loving homes, which sometimes is easier for unwanted cats than books. After all, if the books were useful in the first place, the library would not be getting rid of them.

Because books are physical objects, they are also perishable. Mold, deterioration, fires, disintegration all threaten the immortality of the library book. Though an idealized library triumphing over time, space, and mold spores is imagined, it is just that—an ideal rather than a reality.

Even in those libraries where space and physical deterioration are not problems, ever-changing electronic resources make the permanent recording of information challenging. Ownership versus access remains a central concern for libraries. Given the unstable corporate environment of many information providers, librarians are rightfully skeptical about entrusting the commercial world with their sacred duty to maintain and preserve their written legacy. But in some subject areas there are few realistic alternatives. The print versions may be exorbitantly priced. Space may not be available to house these resources, even if they can be physically acquired. Accelerating price increases also keep libraries from purchasing and owning many key titles.

The sheer amount of information being produced limits the ability of libraries to adequately acquire, organize, preserve, and disseminate the written knowledge of civilization. Thomas Cahill said, "History proves nothing because it contains everything."[27] Referring to religions' directives to remember, Harvey Cox observes that "to remember everything is to remember nothing in particular. One would be better off to forget."[28] Underscoring the problem of too much information coming in, Jorge Luis Borges wrote a story titled "Funes el Memorioso" in which a riding accident causes a man to remember every minute of every day, all conversation and all his thoughts, even remembering remembering. The act of remembering comes to consume him, leaving time for nothing but remembering.

And so it seems that libraries must spend an inordinate amount of time, effort, and money controlling the overwhelming production of information. Still, in reality, they do accomplish this task. Though by no means a perfect system, libraries are still able to acquire books, organize them, share information about their holdings, and provide the materials to those who need them.

If they didn't, no one would lug boxes of books to donate them to libraries. Whether real or imagined, authors still seek their immortality through library shelves, and they do so for good reason. Libraries provide them, if not immortality, at least longevity beyond their physical years on earth. An analysis of the 1800s Charleston library collection found several books still on the shelf today. And when the temples and royal palaces of the Tigris and Euphrates valleys were excavated, "Houses of Tablets" were found attached to these ancient religious and governmental seats of power. Even with the ability to ensure their legacies through pyramids and mummification, the written word still was seen as one of the best methods to provide life everlasting.

NOTES

1. Cox, *Common Prayers*, 58.
2. As discussed in Sterling, "Evolution," 102.
3. Tocqueville and Commager as quoted in Brooks, *On Paradise Drive*, 95, 98.
4. Douglas, *City*, 516.
5. Battles, *Library*, 6.
6. As quoted in Griliches, *Library*, 70, 31, 45.
7. Lerner, *Forest for the Trees*, 189.
8. Battles, *Library*, 193.
9. Moyers, *Moyers on America*, 50.
10. Wolfe, *Transformation*, 97.
11. As quoted in Tolzmann et al., *Memory of Mankind*, xi.
12. Susman, *Culture as History*, 290.
13. Rosen, *Joy Comes in the Morning*, 24.
14. Lerner, *Forest for the Trees*, 184, 230.
15. As quoted in ibid., 231.
16. Moyers, *Moyers on America*, ix, x.
17. As quoted in Griliches, *Library*, 65 (emphasis added).
18. Battles, *Library*, 136.
19. Ibid., 119.
20. Ibid., 207, 209.
21. Battelle, "Birth of Google," 106.
22. Thompson, "Scriptoria," 146.
23. Manguel, *History of Reading*, 50.
24. "History of Scriptoria," Oct. 18, 2004. http://www.christdesert.org/noframes/script/history.html.
25. Babylonian Talmud, Tractate Megillah 15a.
26. Grafton, *Footnote*, 5.
27. Cahill, *How the Irish*, 5.
28. Cox, *Common Prayers*, 162.

CHAPTER FIVE

Librarians and Libraries Uplift Individuals and Society

sk any librarian what is the first thing they hear when approached at the reference desk, and they will tell you it is a confession. "It's been a long time since I have used a library," or "I know I should know how to do this," are murmured by library users before they dare even ask where the restroom is. Haughty librarians of yore exploited these penitential offerings by following each confession with a sneer, which may explain why libraries used to be so quiet. People were too ashamed to speak. But now modern librarians indoctrinated in the dogma of customer service immediately absolve the guilt-ridden with an understanding, "Of course," or "That's okay," resulting in a more relaxed, if noisier, library patron.

One need not even come to the library to suffer library guilt. Like religious service attendance, survey respondents consistently exaggerate library usage. If all the people who say they attend church "daily or weekly" and those who report using their local libraries "often or frequently" actually did so, both institutions would exceed the "Maximum Capacity" signs posted in their buildings several times over.

People may enter the library already feeling guilty, but librarians inadvertently perpetuate their shame through the ubiquitous "READ" posters plastered on library walls. In these graven images, bigger-than-life movie icons sit serenely with books splayed upon their laps and dispense beatific smiles to all who pass below. Where churches place a picture of Jesus and the Bible, libraries display a photo of Britney Spears with her copy of *Harry Potter and the Sorcerer's Stone.* "PRAY," demands the felt banner on the wall in a church. "READ," implores Oprah Winfrey in the reference room. One different four-letter word spells the path to salvation in both locales.

"Develop Yourself" is a recent variation on this theme. From superimposed photos of friendly faces and camera film on posters and bookmarks, the implied message is that personal fulfillment will come in the library through exposure—so to speak—to books.

Operating in a secular environment, librarians may not realize the subtle religious message of these campaigns. But there is no doubt about it; the "READ" campaigns are part of an underlying redemptive mission that is nothing short of the secular version of evangelization. The word "evangelical" comes from the Greek word for the good news of the Gospel. The primary obligation of evangelicals is to save as many souls as possible. Librarians also want to spread the "good news," but theirs is not the word of the Gospel but rather the words of all gospels. Or, more specifically, they bring the gospel of words. Fundamental to librarians is the assumption that one will be "delivered" to a better place through reading.

The use of guilt in libraries to encourage individual self-improvement is part of a larger redefinition of the concept of sin and salvation. Organized religions once held the monopoly on redeeming individuals from sin by employing what Harvard theologian Harvey Cox dubbed "moral terrorism."[1] Religious institutions would frighten people with threats of everlasting punishment. Attending church, eating certain food, performing ritual acts, uttering magical incantations could bring blessed redemption, while failing to do these things or doing them incorrectly could spell dire consequences. No matter what someone had done wrong, religion was the authority setting and enforcing the rules for salvation.

RETHINKING SIN AND SALVATION

The traditional understanding of sin and salvation no longer characterizes the mind-set of most people; a different version has arisen in its place. Indeed, one minister quipped that, "when we use words 'redemption' or 'conversion,' people think we're talking about bonds." Belief that sinners will be eternally damned, or that they must repent in order to be eternally redeemed, describes the religious outlook of few Americans. According to surveys of religious thought, among all major American religions the hell-and-damnation sense of sin no longer holds sway. "Any religion that demands you believe in human depravity won't make it in America," concluded religion scholar Alan Wolfe. The de-emphasis of sin and salvation has not been limited to the major liberal Protestant and Jewish denominations. Even fundamental denominations have changed their stance on this once-central doctrine. One survey found that only 16 percent of Southern Baptist Church sermons included the classic image of fire and damnation.[2]

The Lord to whom most Americans, including many born-again Christians, turn today rarely gets angry. Within American Christianity, the formerly central traditional teachings about heaven and hell, sin and the devil have lost their saliency for many and fallen away entirely for others. Within American Catholicism there has been a noted decrease in the rite of confession. Indicative of the changed perspective, even the Catholic Church has softened its fire-and-brimstone vision of hell. Pope John Paul II referred to hell as a symbol of spiritual isolation. Rather than flames and demons with tridents, the pontiff equated eternal damnation with the pain of realizing that one is cut off from what makes life livable.[3]

Free Choice

Fear of eternal damnation may no longer influence religious believers as it once did, but a deeply held belief in individual free choice remains strong. Central to the belief system of most Americans is the notion that an individual can alter his or her station in life—be it financially or morally—by what they do here and now. The idea of predestined fate holds little attraction within American thought. The bootstraps mentality stressing individual control is alive and well. As the ad slogan puts it, "Just Do It." Those who "do it" will be rewarded, those who don't have only themselves to blame. Cox reminds us that Christianity and Judaism insist that human beings are created with the freedom to examine their lives and, with the help of God, mend their ways. Though we are bound by our time, place, and genetic inheritance, what we do is up to us.[4]

Americans fervently believe that individuals are responsible for their actions and will be rewarded or punished because of them. It is up to us—and not a religious organization—to improve ourselves. Replacing the former belief in divine intercession, self-fulfillment and self-improvement are now the true avenues to contemporary salvation. As Northwestern University media professor Laura Kipnis puts it, "Once brimstone and hellfire kept populations in line, now there's sudsy self-improvement."[5]

The contemporary emphasis on self-improvement brings to mind the biblical Hebrew word for sin, *chait*, which was derived from the archery term meaning to miss the mark. Human frailty was understood as the individual striving for perfection but not quite hitting the target straight on every time. Today both the creation of the target and one's progress toward it are up to each person.

Psychology of Sin

When the pope refers to hell as a symbol of spiritual isolation rather than a fiery pit, obviously a profound change in the religious imagination is at work. Like the pope, people have retreated from the former notion of sin, adopting instead nonjudgmental language of wrongdoing. Religion experts call this transformation the "psychologizing" of American religion. People today seek "well-being" rather than deliverance. Cultural historian Jackson Lears sees the trend as a switch from Protestantism to secularity, salvation to self-realization.[6] Wolfe sees it as blending the themes of personal recovery with spiritual regeneration.[7]

Ever since the days of Freud there has been a complicated relationship between religion and psychology, at times complementing and at times competing with each other. Throughout most of history, the prescription for curing what we now call psychological problems would have been ascetic prayer, fasting, or religious commitment. But now the source of salvation would more likely be found by making an appointment with a mental health counselor or checking out the latest Wayne Dyer book.

Many theologians have speculated on the reasons for the demise of the previously held doctrine of hell and damnation. The Enlightenment, widespread literacy, increased education, and technological and scientific advances have been proposed as reasons that fear of eternal punishment no longer inspires people's behavior. One hypothesis posits that fewer and fewer Catholics go to confession because they are not as inclined to think of themselves as sinners in the first place.

Pervasive Guilt

Ironically, though the pathway to paradise appears easier, its attainment is more complicated. When salvation required believing in a saving Jesus and going to church on Sunday, the actions one needed to perform were straightforward. But now both the actions and thoughts needed to bring deliverance are murkier. Some believe that this amorphous sense of sin has heightened people's underlying sense of guilt. We aren't quite sure what we should be doing but are vaguely aware that, whatever it is, we're not doing it enough, or correctly, or with the appropriate mind-set. The result is pervasive guilt, which can be manifested in a variety of ways, including an overwhelming desire to confess.

Scholars of religion and popular culture have noted an increased fascination with public television confessions, taking the form of debasing, self-effacing revelations on talk shows. Why someone would come before a nationally televised audience to reveal one's infidelity with their mother-in-law seems incomprehensible. But when seen as a substitution for the rite of confession, it seems at least a bit more understandable, though still bizarre. Likewise, there has been an explosion of television shows that elicit a confession of guilt after intense, belabored police interrogations. The popularity of *The Apprentice* with the thunderous Donald Trump pronouncing the death sentence of "You're fired!" may be seen as a secularized version of a divine decree of damnation, eternally banishing the sinner from the corporate Garden of Eden.

Redefined Contemporary Sins

We no longer worry about saving our eternal souls. Rather, generalized anxiety about obesity, health, love, and money bedevil us today. The American obsession with fat is a prime example of the conflagration of consumer culture, therapeutic remedies, and reimagined sin. Fat has been demonized, claims Dinitia Smith in a *New York Times* article. Historians and cultural critics are beginning to see that the American obsession with obesity is based less on science and more on morality. We feel guilty about the abundance of food and excesses of our consumer culture. Some social critics claim dieting fads are a new kind of puritanism, with dieting becoming a way to express virtue and self-control.[8]

Not only is dieting virtuous but, in the extreme, abstaining from food becomes The Way to ultimate salvation. "Control of your destiny lies in your spoon," proclaims one diet ad. An exercise program promises that by transforming your body you can transform your life. "Only a layer of cellulite stands between [the individual] and bliss," observes Judith Wright, author of *There Must Be More Than This*.[9] "If only I could get thin," the average overweight American thinks, "then I'll feel good about myself." And feeling good about oneself is required for—if not the definition of—personal salvation.

Closely allied to the cult of thinness is the contemporary obsession with health. Rather than praying, fasting, belonging, or believing, the blessing of a long, prosperous, happy life is attainable through diet and exercise. To ensure longevity you must eat the right (i.e., "virtuous") foods, avoid "sinful" temptations, and take care of your body. People used to go to Mass to ward off evil; now they eat tofu and work out at the gym. Certain foods have even taken on an aura of sanctity, while others convey depravity. "Sinful" rich desserts are guaranteed to bring punishment later, while abstinence ensures a blessed long life. David Brooks noted a near-holy feeling in a Whole Food grocery store where he fantasized setting off alarms by smuggling in a bag of Doritos.

The state of medical care is an excellent example of how people become simultaneously more empowered and more confused by relocating both the path to salvation and salvation itself from organized religion to the individual. Individuals are urged to take responsibility for their own health. Not only must you get a second opinion on any medical treatment, but with the "help" of television ads and commercials you must also select your own doctor, decide which hospital is best for you, know which drug to ask your doctor about, and inform yourself about treatment options.

Love with just the right person will also bring about personal salvation. As Kipnis explains, "Just as earlier strivers and pilgrims sought grace and afterlife salvation . . . we subjugate ourselves . . . hoping for similar payoffs here on earth: the salvation of a better relationship."[10]

The attainment of financial success operates as the yardstick of judgment for many people. "Success means what salvation once meant," claims religion historian Peter Gardella. "Millions who practice no organized religion (and millions who do) call themselves to regular internal judgments on the basis of their standards for success."[11] In our consumer culture, money—or the lack thereof—often becomes the measure of an individual's success. Much like obesity, poverty becomes a moral failing because the individual is imagined to be in control. If you fail to attain the expected level of financial well-being— the right kind of house, car, or college for your kid—surely you must have done something wrong.

Even those who refuse to equate their balance sheet with personal success can create other demons with which they torture themselves. Gardella admitted that the production of published books became his own driving ambition. Though he was not proud of it, it became the measure of that man. As a fellow writer, I well understand his torment. My obsessive preoccupation with this writing project is wreaking havoc with my family, but I am bedeviled to persevere. Perhaps this is what demonic possession feels like.

When sin was governed by organized religion, the path to personal redemption was more straightforward; what an individual needed to do, say, or believe was known. Whether they did so or not, at least the road to redemption was obvious. With salvation more a psychological failing, and guilt pervasive, the way out seems less clear. As mentioned, many seek the mental health route and consult a shrink. Others go on yet another diet or join yet another health club. Some, however, head to the library as their source of salvation.

LIBRARIES AND SALVATION

The previous brief detour into redefined sin may seem far removed from librarianship, but it is not. Librarians receive confessions of guilt continually. Exactly what the library penitent feels guilty about, and what exculpatory expression is expected from the librarian, is not clear. Perhaps library users, like many in our society, are plagued with a generalized guilt because of this diffused religious path to salvation. They know they should be improving themselves but are not sure exactly how to go about it. They feel guilt at their ignorance yet at the same time vaguely aware that the library holds the source of their salvation.

It is hard to think of any difficulty plaguing a human being that could not be lessened with the help of a reference librarian. With the plethora of self-help books in existence, most likely a book has been written to help people deal with whatever troubles them, whether the problem be real or imagined. The library is an excellent resource for self-improvement, self-fulfillment, and self-help of all types.

Of course, the library is not the only place people seek help. An entire self-help industry including psychologists, counselors, and mental health services has emerged, each promising their own version of deliverance. Likewise, the consumer market has been more than willing to fill the void by developing aids in the form of books, videos, and products that offer salvation. All of these stand ready to redeem and save people, albeit at a price.

Libraries are unique dispensers of self-help because library assistance is free. Libraries are one of the last bastions of free service. At no cost—if they return their materials on time—library users from the affluent suburban housewife to the homeless drug addict can seek self-improvement without laying out even one penny. The dispensation of library self-help takes various forms: books, online resources, support group meeting space, social service directories, information and referral services. Regardless of the form or format, all library help is free.

But beyond providing self-improvement in the form of self-help guidance, libraries also support those with more philosophical questions. When people need answers to those eternal questions—the reason for suffering, the meaning of life, why bad things happen to good people and vice versa—the library stands ready to help. Books can provide the deep questions and the answers people have asked and answered for thousands of years. Even when the search to answers leads nowhere, solace may be found in knowing that throughout human history people have grappled—sometimes unsuccessfully—with the same questions. But at least they tried.

One book not only offered philosophical pondering, it even spared a life. While being held captive by an accused killer, hostage Ashley Smith began reading from the book *The Purpose-Driven Life*, concentrating on the section that discusses how life is meant to be spent in service to God and others. Her captor asked her to read it again and shortly thereafter set her free.

Library "Flashlight" God

Those with a religious predilection may see these life-affirming aspects of library usage in spiritual terms. For them, a library-dwelling God could be imagined as the divine force that helps one find his or her proper destination. God as Guide, God as Light, or God as The Way all point to this side of the divine that helps people go from the dark place where they are to a brighter spot. In his survey of contemporary religious thought, Wolfe found this notion so prevalent he came to call it the "flashlight" God, the sense that the divine gently guides people toward their individual salvation.[12] By having their paths illuminated, people are provided at least one way toward their individual courses of action.

If God is a "flashlight," for many the source of that shining light is knowledge. It is no coincidence that the scientific revolution was called the Enlightenment, for knowledge and understanding have often been referred to as illumination. When Lady Wisdom walked among the people she carried a torch, bringing light to humanity. Libraries are both the source and storehouse of enlightened knowledge.

Library God as the Force

Along with God as a Guide, others imagine God as the source of individual initiative. "God helps those who help themselves" approximates this expression of this divinity. Not only does God guide, God also inspires. "God only gives you what you can handle" is familiar to many. Or, as Nietzsche put it, "What does not kill me, makes me stronger." In contemporary theology, God becomes the *ability* to handle what is put before you, the spiritual presence that inspires and supports action. For Christians this aspect of holiness can be found in the Holy Spirit or grace; for Jews, the Torah; for Eastern religions, karma. Described succinctly in popular theology as "God is a verb," the ability to deal with life's triumphs and failures is imagined as divinely inspired, if not divine itself. Moviegoers will recognize the *Star Wars* sort of God: "May the force be with you" is a prayer of inspiration and hope. Poet Ruth Brin beautifully describes this divine force as "the strength of life, the power moving us to do good, the source of love."[13]

Especially important for American society, which emphasizes the individual over community, God can also be seen as the force that brings people together. Feminists have seized on this and added feminine images to describe God. "Life force," "breath of life," "wellspring" are all meant to capture the pervasiveness and beauty of this aspect of God. The walk-in-the-woods God found in nature, usually engendered as Mother Nature, borders on this divine notion, but the Force is more than the sum total of the natural world.

Obviously God as Force, or God as Guide, can be located within the library setting. God can be seen not only as the force that brought a person to the library but also that which sustains them to continue searching. (Given the high frustration levels associated with computer searching, divine assistance is often needed to persevere.) God can also be seen as that which guides people in their quest, whether they are seeking help to lose weight, find a better job, or discover the ultimate meaning of life. As Mark Edmundson notes in a book aptly titled *Why Read?* the world is full of "farmers, tradesmen and tradeswomen, mechanics, lawyers, and, up to some crucial moment, layabouts, who've used books to turn their lives around."[14] Of course, for those on outright religious journeys, the library can also be a natural setting for exploring the relational aspect of God.

But no matter what subject brings someone to the library, the process of using a library can be seen as a secularized version of salvation. The person comes into the library because of some acknowledged lack or need, believing the answer will be found there. In the Bible people were invited: "Seek and ye shall find; knock and the door will be opened to you" (Mt 7:7). A similar invitation could be made at the library. Here you will find what you need, with the help of an imagined or believed divine presence, possibly serving as a guide or force to help in your search.

History of Library Salvation

Well before the self-actualization, self-help era began in the 1960s, libraries had taken as their mission the lofty goal of improving individuals and society. For librarians deliverance to the promised land of enlightenment can be achieved through reading. The word "library" derives from the Latin *liber*, meaning free. American slaves were forbidden from learning to read because of the power that came with the act. Roman slaves were allowed to learn practical subjects such as math and engineering but were forbidden from reading literature, history, or philosophy for fear learning these "liberal" arts might inspire them to unite and rise up.

Librarians are obviously aware of reading's power. Literacy initiatives have been, and continue to form, a key aspect of library service. Going beyond simply encouraging reading, librarians have historically encouraged what they considered to be "right" reading. Bemoaning the public's demand for stories, librarians at one time strenuously tried to divert them to "worthier" forms of reading. Scorning popular demand, they waged what has been dubbed the "fiction wars." Librarians tried to shape patron tastes from the "cheap and tawdry reading of novels and newspapers toward a redeeming vision of high literary culture."[15] This uplifting-through-right-reading philosophy continued at least into the 1970s when I was in library school. Heated debates about the appropriateness of Nancy Drew mysteries in the children's section exemplified the continuing belief that "wrong reading" can bring dire consequences.

The effort to uplift the masses with right reading actually predates the establishment of American public libraries. Library historian Matthew Battles dates the beginning of the saving mission of libraries to the nineteenth century, when librarians' role went from being "largely custodial to that of caregiver." As keeper of the books—their original mission—the librarian saw his (and it usually was a male) primary duties as "counting the books, fetching them, and . . . returning them to the shelves." By the turn of the century, though, librarians had become "the information social workers of modernity." Also called "intellectual physicians," librarians would diagnose and treat readers' aberrations.[16]

One of the first efforts to uplift the masses in America began in the 1900s and was a precursor to the public library movement in this country. Librarians would deliver a "home library"—consisting of a cupboard stuffed with as few as twenty books—to rural readers and settlement houses. A librarian or volunteer would deposit the chest of books and return in a week or so to collect them, discuss them, and offer another set of selections. The acknowledged power and respect that emanated from this piece of furniture was at times palpable. This shrine to knowledge was often positioned proudly in people's living rooms or parlors. One writer even likened the bookcase to "an altar filling the room with the glow of books." The aim of these home libraries, which eventually became bookmobiles, was undeniably social uplift. As Battles put it, home libraries and the settlement-house outreach program were designed "to bring untutored masses into the circle of readers, to set them on a path to right reading that would lead from adventure stories to travel to tales to geography, history and the trades."[17]

In the early 1900s, libraries also played a key role in "Americanizing" newly arrived immigrants to this country. One 1920 Carnegie study of Americanization efforts at the time found that "amongst all the institutions in American life, libraries had achieved the best results." Librarians will be proud to know that libraries managed this task without "de-racializing, divesting, remodeling or otherwise 'Americanizing' immigrants; rather, libraries interested immigrants in American life by first interesting themselves in the life of the immigrant."[18] Branch libraries were especially successful in serving as community centers for immigrant neighborhoods. Along with supplying books in foreign languages and providing easy-to-read books, libraries also conducted English classes and assisted users in obtaining citizenship.

Beyond these services, some of which are still offered today, libraries also served their immigrant populations with innovative programs. In his survey of historical library service to immigrants, Eric Novotny found reports of librarians writing condolence letters, naming babies, and loaning soap to "ragged and dirty school children." Novotny grants that an undercurrent of paternalism can be found in some library efforts on behalf of immigrants, but he concluded that librarians generally provided services with "sympathy and understanding" and "an appreciation for the contributions immigrants made to American life."[19]

Along with intellectual and moral uplift, libraries promised their patrons other virtues as well. Melvil Dewey hoped an efficiently run library would promote "efficiency in readers' lives." John Stuart Mill believed libraries offered happiness, repose, and reflection. Charles Dickens "was confident libraries would teach that capital and labour are not opposed, but mutually dependent and mutually supporting."[20] More recently, Philadelphia Judge Matthew D. Carrafiello issued an injunction blocking that city from reducing library hours because such an action would pose irreparable harm to the city. "The local library is one of the strongest antidotes to the drug culture and violence affecting Philadelphia's children," claimed Judge Carrafiello.[21]

Libraries and Societal Redemption

Most of the discussion above has focused on personal salvation. But societal improvement was also central to the library saving mission, albeit usually one person at a time. Though most think of sin as an individual's actions against God, societal improvement depends on the actions of individuals, as a simple story can suggest:

After living through the horrors of the holocaust and watching his best friend die of cancer, an old man angrily cries to God: "There is so much pain and anguish in the world, God. Why don't you send help?"

"I did send help," God answers. "I sent you."

Individuals organized and inspired through religions have been instrumental in bringing about societal justice. Many credit Christianity with abolishing slavery in America. The Catholic social movement was instrumental in the establishment of a myriad of social programs of the Progressive era. The Jewish prophetic tradition of social justice is credited with correcting countless injustices throughout history. In *The Gifts of the Jews*, Thomas Cahill credits Judaism for awakening civilization to the possibility that tomorrow can be different, and therefore better than today.

Especially after the Enlightenment and scientific revolution, there existed a sense that everything—both personal and communal—was redeemable through knowledge. By combining individual freedom and scientific progress, communal salvation seemed within reach. As Francis Bacon put it, even the fall of Adam and Eve was reversible through "thought and its products."

Like religion, libraries have been active proponents of social change. Libraries have been intimately involved in freeing individuals, even if it was freeing only their minds through knowledge and books. In compiling a book of essays on the library vision of the future, editor Gregg Sapp noted the library profession's "passionate commitment to democracy and societal improvement." The essays also revealed that the library's role in educating and improving society formed a common theme in futuristic writings.[22]

The possibility of societal improvement can be seen as a foundational belief of libraries. As Battles put it, "Librarians believed in the unlimited possibility of the library for the reformation of culture and society." It was assumed not only that right reading could enlighten an individual but that an educated, enlightened populace could bring about a better society. For instance, John Stuart Mill said that library books "offered a greater good than reason." These books would "ultimately encourage the regard for one's fellow man" and form the foundation of altruism.[23]

Even now libraries continue their central role in maintaining democracy in this country. The National Issues Forum, which aims to improve the quality of civic discourse, is convening library-based public forums about thorny public policy issues. The library was chosen as the site for this program to heal a societal ill: polarization and partisan gridlock. "Libraries can prove the antidote," explained the initiative founder, LBJ Presidential Library and Museum's Taylor Willingham.[24]

Libraries as Violent Liberators

The Library as Liberator may seem an odd concept to those who picture libraries as refuges from the world at large. Libraries are thought of as safe sanctuaries far removed from the dangers and evils all around. Yet libraries are also powerful, potentially dangerous places. This library power exists both in the potentially destabilizing potential of its contents and the authority vested in those who control access to it. To understand the latter, consider how librarians have been portrayed historically. Librarians were scary individuals. Scowling, mean, able to inspire fear with a mere eyebrow, these austere individuals were frightening. Not exactly thought of as witches, they were close to it. The awe-inspiring librarians were dangerous because the power they wielded was none other than the accumulated knowledge of civilization.

When the right information was applied at the right time in the right amount in the right circumstances, library knowledge could be devastating. Kings could be toppled, revolutions begun, slaves set free. Knowledge is power may seem a cliché, but it is far from trivial. Librarians and libraries have the power to change not only lives but the course of history. If that is not a liberator, what is?

The saving mission of libraries through reading usually brings to mind a gentle, benign path to personal salvation, but at times library salvation has been imagined through violence. For instance, in 1935 German librarians adopted the slogan "The Book—A Sword of the Spirit" for their annual Book Week celebration, though they later retreated from this campaign when it was used malevolently by the Nazis.

Realizing the potential for books to radically alter one's outlook on life, Kafka called books "the ice ax of the soul," an image far removed from one of a placid, gentle reader.

Libraries and books have been credited with liberating enslaved people. Victor Hugo said that when Gutenberg invented movable type it "marked the transition of man-slave to the free-man." Echoing the liberating power of libraries, Malcolm X said,

> I had never been so truly free in my life as when in the prison library. Ten guards and the warden couldn't have torn me out of those books. Months passed without even thinking about being imprisoned. . . . I don't think anybody ever got more out of going to prison than I did.[25]

Perhaps one of the best descriptions of the library enabling personal triumph was offered by Henry Louis Gates Jr.:

> In tenth grade, when I was fourteen, I had a friend who played chess a lot. I thought, I'm better at games than all the rest of the kids, so I'm going to play this guy and beat him. He crushed me. It was ugly. Then one day when I was at the library, I came across a book on chess . . . it was love at first sight. . . . That's when I discovered that reading could open your mind to the wonders of everything you wanted to know. For the first time, I understood the power of books, because after I started reading them, I began crushing players I couldn't beat before.[26]

Liberating God

Just as God the Force and God the Light can be imagined in a library setting, God as Liberator can be seen within a library context. The empowering righteousness experienced above—allowing players to be beaten and crushed—approximates one of my favorite images of God. Depicted perfectly by Sally Field in the movie *Norma Rae*, the hero stands atop a table in an intolerable sweatshop, thrusting a poster overhead demanding one word: "UNION!" Here is the biblical prophetic voice of God, proclaiming justice and righting wrongs here on earth, the superhuman-conquering-evil version of the divine. This prophetic voice of God combats institutional social injustice such as slavery, financial inequity, and racial and ethnic hatred.

This aspect of God is perhaps the only matter most religious Americans seem to agree upon. Social critic Robert Bellah says the prophetic voice of American public life "to carry out God's will on earth" has been a characteristic of American thought since the days of Puritan New England.[27] Liberation theology, founded to right injustices prevalent in Latin America, typifies this kind of God. God not only helps those in poverty but also questions the root causes of poverty.

Closely allied to the liberating God is the frightening God. The meek, benevolent, peaceful God may inspire love but seems inadequate to confront factory owners or slaveholders. Known in the Bible as the wrath of God, this dimension of the divine can be seen as Yahweh thundering from Mt. Sinai, drowning the Egyptian army, reigning "destruction upon those who oppress the helpless and grind down the poor." This second side of the holy, called *mysterium tremendum et fascinans* by theologian Rudolf Otto, has been depicted for thousands of years in different religious traditions. In Hinduism the god Kali is seen as the "malicious face of the divine, with a belt of dismembered arms and necklace of skulls." Buddhist, especially Tibetan, iconography employs dreadful and grotesque images of deities.[28]

American religions scholar Cheryl Bridges Johns has noted the demise of such wrathful images of God. Studying grassroots religious movements in the United States, Johns uncovered a trend to "remold God into the most pleasant and obliging deity imaginable." God is now merciful, benevolent, or what Cox has dubbed the "oh-so-nice God." No one shudders in its presence, for this reimagined divinity is now "a user-friendly God." Cox, Otto, and others have argued that, even though religions have toned down images of the powerful, awe-inspiring God, there remains a place for such an image within the human heart.[29]

A place for such an image can also be found within the library. It is true that libraries help people individually by helping each move from where they are to a better place. But combined social action can also deliver entire groups of people to a better place. As discussed above, libraries have been key players in social justice movements. Believers may see God the Liberator as present in the library, providing not just knowledge to users but the inspiration to act on what they learn.

Other Library Sins

Because of their potential to deliver salvation and violence, librarians do not take their service lightly. Indeed, arguably one value librarians hold in common is the belief that withholding library service from any individual or group of potential users is a sin. Librarians today look back in horror at the Jim Crow period, when "some people were unsuited to be readers." Libraries delivered "unbearable pain" by withholding library service.[30]

Closely allied to the sin of withholding library service is another action librarians consider sinful: desecrating books. Though appalling to librarians, this act is nothing new. In 1725 Thomas Hollis (of Harvard Library fame) wrote, "Students take [books] to their chambers, and teare out pictures & maps to adorn their Walls, such things are not good."[31]

Of course, the public is well aware of one other form of library sinning, requiring pennies rather than penance. The fine for overdue materials does provide financial support for libraries, though it may arrive at a rate of only five cents per day, per item, per sinner. Though it usually does not amount to much money for libraries, it does increase library guilt, which most suffer already by simply walking through the library doors.

NOTES

1. Cox, *Common Prayers*, 214.
2. As quoted in Wolfe, *Transformation*, 91, 175, 168.
3. Cox, *Common Prayers*, 214.
4. Ibid., 46.
5. Kipnis, *Against Love*, 69.
6. As discussed in Prothero, *American Jesus*, 91.
7. Wolfe, *Transformation*, 182–83.
8. Smith, "Demonizing Fat," A15–A17.
9. As quoted in Skenazy, "When Skinny Means Happy."
10. Kipnis, *Against Love*, 69.
11. As quoted in Pahl, *Shopping Malls*, 106.
12. Wolfe, *Transformation*, 165.
13. "A Woman's Meditation," in *Kol Haneshamah: Prayerbook for the Days of Awe*, Elkins Park, PA: Reconstructionist Press, 1999, 456.
14. Edmundson, *Why Read?* 32.
15. Battles, *Library*, 120.
16. Ibid., 120, 152, 154.
17. Ibid., 197, 198.
18. Novotny, "Library Services," 349.
19. Ibid., 346–48.
20. As quoted in Battles, *Library*, 137.
21. "Judge Blocks Philadelphia Library from Making Additional Cuts," April 8, 2005. www.ala.org.
22. Sapp, *Brief History*, xxi, xvii.
23. Battles, *Library*, 120; Mill as quoted in, 137.
24. "Interview: Straight Answers from Taylor Willingham," *American Libraries*, April 2005: 23.
25. As quoted in Griliches, *Library*, 77, 32–33.
26. Gates, *America Behind*, 7.
27. As quoted in Nathanson, *Over the Rainbow*, 269.
28. Cox, *Common Prayers*, 26, 27.
29. Johns as quoted in ibid., 27; see also 209.
30. Battles, *Library*, 180.
31. Ibid., 85–86.

CHAPTER SIX

Libraries Provide Sacred, Secular Space

*L*ibraries are inherently schizo-phrenic institutions. They are paradoxically public private spaces. This mixed-up role can be seen in the reasons people come to libraries. According to a major study of library usage, people give two major reasons for visiting libraries: to read and to check out books.[1] At first glance this seems so obvious as to be laughable. Of course people go to libraries to read. To paraphrase the bank robber's selected target, that's where the books are. But unlike any bank robbers I know, people also do the reverse; they bring their own books *to* the library.

Why, one wonders, don't they just stay home if they want to read? Or why don't they head to a park or nearby café? To engage in the very private activity of reading, many people prefer the public library setting, even if they already have the reading material in hand.

The reason they prefer this location is even more paradoxical. One of the major draws of the library setting is the presence of others who have come there to read by themselves. All these people come to this public place to be alone with others who want to be alone. Libraries are a place for people to be together separately. Talk about conflicting purposes.

Buried within this ironic use of libraries is the profound, complicated interplay of the library's public and private roles. Amazingly, the institution of the library manages to balance these opposing roles by providing a place to be both alone and with others.

THE LIBRARY'S PARADOXICAL ROLES

Libraries are inherently social organizations. Whether public, academic, school, or special, they are formed communally by a group for the sharing of resources among members (see chapter 7). But libraries also provide for the isolation of individuals from each other. Paradoxically, the library is a communal institution that promotes noncommunal activity. Indeed, it could be argued that one of the key purposes of libraries is to encourage its members to separate themselves from each other and pursue their own private aims.

Why, one may ask, would a community want to provide a public space for private pursuits? The answer lies in the underlying assumption of the social benefit to be derived from individual interests. Each person, it is believed, will emerge from the isolated experience of library use in some enhanced way. Other parts of this book explore how libraries are seen as agents of personal and societal uplift, places where some higher purpose or power seems present. To be more precise, the ancient biblical term "dwells" comes to mind. "Contemplative oasis" is how one person described a college library.

Somehow, just being in the library refreshes the soul, imbuing one with an elusive sense of the sublime. It is no accident that the movie *City of Angels* chose the library as the earthly residence of angels. Indeed, images of angels are frequently associated with libraries. The New York Public Library contains countless statues and paintings of winged emissaries of God. Angels represent the link between the secular and the divine, residing on earth yet somehow separated from it. Like angels, libraries also unite the secular and spiritual. "Libraries are like mountains or meadows or creeks: sacred space," says author Anne Lamott.[2]

For a demonstration of this thesis, consider how people act when they enter a traditional library (one built before 1950). They walk slowly, grow quiet, speak in whispers if they speak at all. Though indescribable, libraries evoke a feeling of goodness, power, and lasting importance that resembles that experienced in an old-fashioned church. An ineffable force seems present within the library walls.

A library media specialist I know reported an example of this experience when she accompanied a group of second-grade schoolchildren on a tour of a college library. As one would expect of a gaggle of children, the group was animated and noisy as they clamored up the entryway stairs of the library. As they came upon the grand expanse of the main reading room, without being told to, the entire class immediately quieted. When they reached the top of the stairs, they stood silently as they studied the expanse of the vaulted ceilings and marble floor of the grand reading room. No one spoke for several minutes, until a boy of about six simply said, "God lives here."

Bookstores Lack Sacred Feeling

The feeling of library sanctification is especially apparent when compared to bookstores. Though sharing a similar purpose, bookstores do not inspire this feeling. This fact was driven home to me as I tried to imagine a joint-use facility between a library and bookstore. Joint-use library facilities—where two different types of institution, such as a community college and a public library, share one library—are prevalent in south Florida. The idea of consolidating a library and bookstore has surfaced here and there—not merely relegating library space for a bookstore but integrating the book selections of both. But the idea never developed. Along with logistical difficulties, such a place could not easily be conjured because of the contradictory feelings between the two. Silence is neither expected nor encouraged from those entering a commercial establishment such as a bookstore. Though libraries and bookstores provide people with an abundant array of information, in bookshops the awe of knowledge does not inspire spiritual sensations. Quite the contrary, bookstores feel like commercial enterprises; they do not feel holy.

Thanks to the science of retail atmospherics, bookstores are designed to produce emotional reactions that enhance purchasing. Specific music, lighting, layout, and color are all chosen with buying in mind. Indeed, in bookstores, rather than communing it is consuming that comes to mind, whether it be reading material or a latte. Retail establishments such as bookstores manipulate smells to entice food purchases, strategically infusing the shopping area with cinnamon, coffee, and apples because they are associated with family and warmth.[3]

In point of fact, it may be the *lack* of food and drink in the library that contributes to its feeling of sanctity. Paco Underhill, an expert on shopping center design, notes that it is hard to think of a public space in America that is not associated with a certain food. "Each has its significant dish," he explains. "Hot dogs at the ballpark (along with peanuts and Cracker Jacks), popcorn at the movies . . . roasted chestnuts on the streets of New York. At the mall you've got the aroma of Cinnabon."[4]

But places of reverence, such as libraries and houses of worship, are lacking such an associative food. Try to think of a library food. In kindergarten I remember Jonathan Harding eating library paste, but that hardly counts as a bibliographic delicacy.

Library as Private Seclusion

It is not only the lack of food that makes a library building feel profoundly different from a commercial establishment. Libraries provide privacy for their users, while bookstores discourage seclusion from others to limit opportunities for shoplifting. Providing opportunities for private, quiet contemplation is central to the library's mission. Because of the aforementioned schizophrenic library usage, people come to the library seeking seclusion from other library users, but they still desire the comfort that comes from knowing that others are nearby. Library carrels, alcoves, cubbies, and separated desks provide this contradictory private spot within a public setting. Many people find a favorite hideaway, be it a comfy chair tucked among the stacks or a certain table in the back of a reading room, claiming it as their own. Like churchgoers who always sit in a certain pew, library users return time and time again to their own special reading nook.

So prized are these separate spots that many academic libraries are forced to devise elaborate regulations to ration the use of their cagelike pens in the stacks. With their chain-link fences these enclosures often resemble jail cells. From their austere appearance, one would assume they would create a feeling of imprisonment. But the faculty adore these spaces, often fighting fiercely for the right to inhabit them. Not only are the spaces useful, they can also feel warm and coddling. Historian Barbara Tuchman credits being given "one of those little cubicles with a table under a window" as the single most formative experience that led to her becoming a writer.[5]

Library space is also attractive because the library is one of the only public institutions where one can escape a feeling of being watched. Philosopher Michel Foucault observed—long before September 11—that in modern enclosures such as factories, schools, barracks, and prisons, people are constantly "supervised, processed, subjected to inspection, order and the clock."[6] Foucault's statement is even more accurate today, given the heightened security measures. Though the PATRIOT Act has made users aware of the possibility of intrusion into their private library use, by and large people still feel comfortable and beyond the watch of others when they are in the library.

Comfort in Crowds

Though they want to be alone, library users also want to know others are around. Author Alfred Kazin expressed this succinctly in explaining why he chose the New York Public Library as his preferred location for writing: "I liked reading and working out my ideas in the midst of that endless crowd walking in and out. I took comfort knowing all of them, like me were . . . looking for Something."[7]

Especially in our isolated, detached society, the presence of others can be welcome. Those who live alone know that the silence of solitude can become intolerable, but in a library silence comforts rather than suffocates (assuming there is any library silence; the matter of silent vs. lively library space is discussed later). Charlotte Simmons, a lonely college freshman in a Tom Wolfe novel, preferred studying in the library rather than her dorm room. As she put it, the library was a setting where "sitting alone didn't seem pathetic."

Like Simmons, most people take comfort in the library setting even though they are not seeking direct interaction with others. Reading, writing, or studying—all private acts—are enhanced with the knowledge that others are present and engaging in the same activities. Perhaps this feeling taps some deep-seated biological need in humans to sense that others are around. It must be remembered that humans are social animals. The physical survival of each individual member depends on the group. Perhaps this explains why people turn on their television or radio when home alone. The sound of other human voices as background noise is soothing, even if there is no physical presence to accompany their sounds. Whether it be the disembodied voice of a television commercial or a reading room study carrel, to paraphrase Barbra Streisand's classic song, people do need people.

Privacy Paramount

Though the presence of other people may draw some to the library, in another contradictory attraction of this public place, people like knowing their public actions will remain private. As Kazin observed, everyone in the crowded library, like him, was looking for Something. Librarians are well aware of the variety of fascinating "Somethings" people seek in libraries. Arthur Schopenhauer once said that successful novelists do not chronicle great events but make small ones interesting. Librarians are privy to thousands of these "interesting small events." In libraries, an infinite variety of small events and dramatic human moments unfold. And whether large or small, trivial or momentous, each is revealed within the confines of strict confidentiality.

Especially since September 11, security needs have encroached on personal privacy in a variety of settings. To the credit of the profession, in the library respect for privacy still reigns supreme. Librarians have jealously protected the confidentiality of patron requests. Library visitors do not know what brings anyone else to this secular, sacred place, nor would anyone dare ask. Is that man at computer #6 searching the welfare department's website? Does the woman in the self-help section need advice on leaving her abusive spouse? Perhaps the man with the medical encyclopedia needs an explanation of the carcinoma he has been diagnosed with. Sometimes matters of gravity bring people to this place. As in a hospital waiting room, anyone who comes here is owed respect and privacy.

SIMILARITY OF CHURCH AND LIBRARY

One other public setting confers respect and privacy to all who are present, a place where people go to be alone with others who are alone. Also like the library, this place is sought by people who want to explore private thoughts within a group setting. This place I am speaking of is a house of worship.

No wonder library and church buildings look so similar. Throughout much of Western history the two buildings were combined. The first known libraries were actually monasteries, with small collections of books stuffed in their choir lofts, niches, and roofs. The carrel still prevalent in libraries today is a direct descendant of these religious places. The word "carrel" originally meant "working niche or alcove" and referred to a monastery cloister area where monks would read and write.

Libraries remained as small collections of books in religious institutions through much of European history. For instance, the University Library of Oxford started with a few chained volumes housed in the church of St. Mary. (In what was surely an innovation at the time, these books were unchained for a brief period. They were immediately pawned, redeemed, put back, and stolen once again. The chains were swiftly reattached to the volumes, where they remained for years to come.) According to library architecture historian Nikolaus Pevsner, it was not until monasteries were abolished that secular libraries developed. Books from these former institutions were transferred to the new secular receptacles. The first totally detached secular library did not appear until 1661.[8]

American public libraries also have their roots firmly planted in religious soil. A 1900 report on the status of libraries, quaintly titled *Public Libraries and Proper Education*, lists many libraries originating from church or parish libraries. An early eighteenth-century Protestant clergyman, Rev. Dr. Thomas Bray, is credited with establishing at least thirty libraries through his post as the church's secretary for the propagation of the Gospel. As directed by his bishop in London, he diligently went upon his mission "to supply all of the English colonies in America with libraries." Many of the church libraries Bray founded were antecedents of New England town libraries.[9]

Reflecting their conjoined history, libraries and houses of worship were often based upon similar architectural structures. Many of the same architects designed both types of buildings and used the same blueprints. The most popular American academic library buildings were superimposed upon the layout of a Greek or Roman temple, with stack layouts often adapted from the traditional Gothic chapel basilica. The University of Virginia's original library drew directly from the Pantheon in Rome, while Brown University's was modeled on the Temple of Diana. When Harvard University architect Richard Bond designed the library building on the site of what is now the Widener Library, he took as his model the chapel at King's College but added a transept to form a more distinct cross. Evidently even a chapel design had to feel more religious when it was transformed into a library. The similarity between library and church went too far, according to critics of the Haverford College Library. When built in 1864, many complained that it looked too much like either a "pagan structure" or an "Episcopal chapel." Likewise, in 1887 William Poole griped that too many libraries looked like the old cathedral or Gothic church–type buildings.

Academic libraries not only looked like churches, they were often housed with or near the college's chapel, a trend that continues on many college campuses today. Brown University put its library beneath the chapel; Yale University and the University of South Carolina placed theirs above. It was not until 1840, when the latter school built a library, that the United States had its first freestanding academic library building.

Silent Library Prayer

Along with their historical connection, libraries and houses of worship also have a common function. In the midst of their church, synagogue, or mosque, people commune with God, imagined as the totality of all the world. Library users engage in a similar activity.

Few librarians or library users would refer to what people do in a library as praying, but according to one common definition of the term that is exactly what it is. Prayer has been defined as "directed intention with a special mental concentration."[10] Others see prayer as "simply focusing of one's attention." Poet May Sarton said that, if you look with absolute attention at almost anything, "something like revelation takes place." Buddhist monk Thich Nhat Hanh believes that, if one concentrates deeply enough, "the distinction between observer and observed disappears and is followed by true insight on the part of the observer."[11]

Libraries are a natural setting for such intense concentration. Though prayer is often done alone, public settings can enhance the effectiveness of the activity. Many religions require this most individualistic of acts be performed in public. Jewish prayer services require a quorum, called a *minyan*, of at least ten participants. Islam calls its believers together five times a day. Jesus said, "Where two or three are gathered together . . . there am I" (Mt 18:20). Religions and libraries understand—and respect deeply—the fact that truth seeking is somehow enhanced by the communal setting.

Public Silence

To be effective, prayer conducted in public requires public silence. Religious historian Thomas Cahill said, "We have only to be quiet and listen, to hear the word of God."[12] The central Jewish prayer, the Shema, begins "Hear, oh Israel," which has been interpreted to mean one must be silent in order to hear the voice of God. Liturgists are well aware of the power silence brings to prayer. Silence punctuates the worship service in many religious traditions. The Catholic communion rite is taken in silence. The high point of the Jewish prayer service, the Amidah, is recited in silence. Muslim prayers alternate between moments of spoken prayer and extended periods of silence. All of these religions acknowledge that, paradoxically, silence facilitates communication among people. As any angry spouse knows, the "silent treatment" communicates plenty. But one can also be silent *with* someone, as you are in a church—or in a library.

Not only does silence enable us to communicate with each other, it also allows us to tune into something much grander. As Parker J. Palmer, an expert on the spirituality of education, explains, when we pray silently we can "hear the whole world's speech and feel the whole world's connections."[13] Within the library context silence enables one to "hear" the speech of others by reading from the written record of civilization, an act of listening to the whole world indeed. No wonder an inscription engraved over the entrance to library reading rooms proclaims, "Here voices are lowered and minds raised."

I fondly remember instructing my own daughter in the etiquette of library silence when she was about three years old. As I accompanied her into the adult section for the first time, I put my finger to my lips and said, "In the grown-up section of a library, we need to whisper."

"Okay," she mouthed to me, complying immediately.

A few paces into the reading room she tugged on my coat hem. I crouched down and she whispered in my ear, "Who's sleeping?"

To this three-year-old, mandatory silence implied the presence of nappers. Granted, as long as there are long-winded sermons and Dostoyevsky novels, there will be sleeping in churches and libraries. But usually this is not the reason one refrains from speaking in these institutions. Spectators at golf and tennis tournaments remain quiet so the players can concentrate on their game. In libraries and churches, silence allows everyone present in the room to concentrate on their own private game, so to speak.

Unfortunately, moments of silence are especially rare in our society. We seem to fear the void it creates within us. Studies have shown that fifteen seconds of silence is about all the average gathering can endure.[14] Even in houses of worship, moments of true silence are scarce. To the chagrin of many parishioners, organ or guitar music accompany all too many moments of silent meditation in church. Lamenting the lack of public quiet, children's author Peter Mandel rues the disappearance of that American icon "the strong silent type"—with an emphasis on the silent part. His fantasy is to keep silent for an entire day, but he fears others would interpret it as a sign of insanity.[15]

As librarians know all too well, libraries of late do not offer the level of silence they once did. With their open, democratic, human-scale architecture, modern library buildings make their inhabitants feel welcome and at ease but rarely quietly humbled. In old-fashioned majestic library buildings, silence would descend upon the occupants automatically. Turn-of-the-century novelist Mary Antin remembers watching even boisterous children voluntarily refrain from speaking when they approached the entrance of the Boston Public Library. "The space itself made their chatter hush." Paul Angle saw even the brashest tourists speak in a whisper when they came into a library.[16]

Libraries built before 1960 relied on silence because their concrete, terrazzo, or marble floors were beautiful but acoustically problematic. Libraries constructed later could take advantage of what has been called "the one new practice that contributed more to the desired study ambience of the library than any other: carpet."[17]

Librarians have tried other architectural features, such as small group study rooms, carrels, and later individual computer stations, in the hopes that the physical layout of the building, rather than their constant shushing, would quiet patrons. But, despite these attempts, success in this endeavor has been limited at best. As we see in chapter 7, the library serves as the center of a community along with being a sanctuary from it. This combination of roles creates within the library setting both the needs for a vibrant bevy of activity and an escape from it. Libraries' success in fulfilling the former was reflected in the results of a 2004 survey by the British National Library for the Blind, which found library users' top auditory annoyances to be cell phones, loud music, and screaming children.[18] Libraries are obviously filling their mission as the buzzing center of social life but often at the expense of their sanctuary role.

Pity the poor soul who comes to the library seeking refuge from crying children, teenagers' music, or chronically ringing telephones, for that is exactly what he finds in the library. People who live alone may come to the library because of oppressive silence in their home, but others come to escape the racket in theirs. Libraries serve as a special kind of sanctuary. "Sanctuary" is a religious term but one frequently applied to libraries. Humanities librarian David Isaacson admits that, although he is not conventionally religious, he finds communing and arguing with texts to be holy activities, or "a special kind of sanctuary."[19]

The use of a religious term for libraries is appropriate because both libraries and churches provide a convenient place for contemplation, a place where the intense, focused concentration that is prayer can occur. Religious believers seek serenity in their houses of worship as an escape from the hustle and bustle of the secular world. Libraries, too, serve this purpose. As sanctuaries of knowledge, libraries are separated from the world but house and allow communion with the world's written record.

FEATURES THAT ENHANCE SPIRITUALITY AND AUTHORITY IN THE LIBRARY

Libraries are often positioned in the geographic center of community life, but they stand ready to provide refuge from it. Much like churches, libraries are prominent public buildings strategically placed in the town center so people can quickly retreat from the noise and confusion of daily life and enjoy a moment of peace and quiet. Reflecting their similar purposes, colleges with churches and libraries usually place them next to or across from each other. The proximity underscores that both buildings are central figures in fulfilling the institution's mission. Both are prominent players in the public square but also serve as refuges from it. Beyond the physical location of the building, architectural and psychological elements contribute to the feeling of holiness of the library.

Architecture

Historically, libraries were built to evoke feelings of awe and grandeur rather than a warm, welcoming feeling. Anyone entering these buildings immediately felt humbled by their greatness. The awesome power of Something Bigger Than Myself would cower stoics and skeptics alike. Libraries built between 1910 and 1945 employed what is known in architecture as monumentality, meaning the size (and cost) of certain features exceeded what was needed functionally. Lofty ceilings, grand expanses, and stained glass windows were deliberately used to inspire religion-like reactions. Grandiose staircases, broad entries, and sumptuous building materials were also used. Actual palaces and cathedrals formed the architectural heritage of many such buildings.

The physical placement of the reference desk in libraries was also used to both confer authority to the librarian and make users cower in her presence. The Princeton Library was the first to provide a central dais as a station for the librarian. In 1873, to underscore his conviction that a "college library should be accessible in the *highest* degree," Frederic Vinton designed an elevated central platform with iron railings for the librarian. The reference platform became a perfect panopticon, which is an arrangement of an interior space allowing all parts to be visible from a single point. Jerry Bentham used this panopticon design for prisons.[20]

Vinton elevated the librarian's station for control over the library domain. It takes little imagination to see how physically elevating the authority figure empowers that person. Throughout history houses of worship centralized and raised their religious symbols and anointed individuals to "lord" over the congregation. Gods reigned from temples built on the tops of mountains. Kings ruled from majestic thrones. Judges dispensed rulings from raised benches. Police maintained order from horses, which heightened both the officer and the terror experienced by the crowd.

Upon entering a Catholic church during Mass and seeing the priest on the altar amid the religious icons, even those not of that faith feel awed and humbled. With a stretch of the imagination (some may say a long stretch), one could experience a similar feeling when seeing librarians dispense knowledge and truth from their towering perches. Though librarians certainly are neither royalty nor gods, physically raising the librarian increases her stature.

The psychological effect of these massive structures and raised platforms could be profound. As Paul Angle put it, standing in a library one knew "what went on here matched the majesty of the surroundings." When in the reading room of the Boston Public Library, author Mary Antin likened the place to a palace, feeling "the grand spaces under the soaring arches as a personal attribute of my being. It seemed a miracle as great as any on record." After photographing a series of sumptuous libraries for a beautiful coffee-table book, photographer Diane Griliches noted, "With their fine woodwork, walls lined with books, bronze lamps, sculpture, and murals, one was surrounded by greatness, a greatness matching the collection of intellectual treasures within."[21]

Aura of Sanctity

Grand architecture alone does not make libraries feel holy. The lack of savory smells does not make churches and libraries feel sacred, nor does the presence of commercial activity by itself make bookstores secular. It takes a combination of elements to create a feeling of holiness. An inexplicable religious sense, a focus on communal values, a feeling of being transported to a different place in time or space, the commemoration of the deceased; these are some of the conditions that lend sanctity to a space. In one way or another, the library setting provides each of these elements.

Cultural anthropologist Clifford Geertz said that the power of the religious experience can be found in religion's "aura of serenity."[22] By creating a certain mood, the person feels as if lifted to a different place. As Geertz rightly realized, the feeling of holiness is predominantly internal. Somehow the person experiences holiness in that space, but it is an aura or mood—internal expressions of emotion—evoked by the physical surroundings.

Harvard theologian Harvey Cox describes having such an emotional experience the first time he entered a European cathedral as a teenager. Upon seeing the light streaming through the stained glass, he grew speechless. "I was hardly able to move my arms and legs. I was not really thinking in the usual sense of the word. What was happening to me was a classical example of what Rabbi Abraham Heschel called the 'preconceptual level.' I have spent decades of my life filling in the theological content."[23]

Though difficult to define, the desire for this experience of the sacred drives much of religious practice. When asked their reason for attending Mass, only 20 percent of Catholics said they came to church to receive the sacraments. Most (37 percent) said they came seeking the "feeling of meditating and communicating with God."[24] In other words, they wanted to experience that elusive aura of holiness.

Focus on Communal Values

Sacred places function as "focusing lenses" by directing attention to ideals a culture holds most dear. For those who stand upon a sacred spot, the values and principles of a community stand out and become real. Not only do these ultimate truths emerge, they also empower people to act upon them. Religion scholars have noted that locations deemed sacred "apparently create a space in which personal and sometimes collective change can occur."[25]

Libraries provide a space for individuals to change. Rarely is knowledge gained without an impact. As people discover and internalize knowledge, they at least contemplate, and frequently act upon, what they learn. Both individual and societal improvements take place regularly within library walls. Freedom, liberation, and feelings of empowerment have all been associated with the learning that occurs in the library.

Libraries by their very nature serve as "focusing lenses" for literate people. Because they contain the written wisdom of civilization, libraries direct the attention of users to what has been committed to paper. Any ideal a culture holds dear gets captured in writing, but not everything that gets written rises to the level of a cultural ideal. Rather, librarians provide the "focusing lenses" to cultural knowledge by taking the time to select, catalog, classify, index, and preserve what the society deems worthy. The importance of any given item emerges once put through this historical filtering process.

Pilgrimage and Feeling Transported to a Different Place

At a sacred space one pays homage to the remembered event, be it mythical or real, associated with that spot. These sacred locations can be either outwardly religious or secular. The Vietnam Veterans Memorial, the Lincoln Memorial, and sites of famous battles have been called sacred, secular spots. Likewise, the meccas of pop culture such as Disney World and Elvis Presley's Graceland have been identified as sacred, secular spots. Some scholars believe movies can serve as religious journeys because they transport those within their midst to another place.[26]

So powerful is the experience of transformation that some religions require believers to visit the physical site of a remembered event to reenact it ritually by their presence. Going to Mecca is one of the Pillars of Islam. Seeing the Wailing Wall can be a religious experience for both observant and nonreligious Jews. In these places one imagines what went on before, relives the experience, and feels transported across time. A "fundamental need" exists, said historian of religion Mircea Eliade, "for the religious person to periodically re-immerse him or herself into a time and place perceived as eternal and inde-structible."[27]

Harvey Cox came to understand the power of sacred sites after visiting Capernaum in Israel: "After years of looking down with condescension on the pious souls who become weepy and mawkish over 'holy places,' I was reduced to tears, my stern Protestant skepticism melting under the Galilean sun." Actually being at the space where fact and myth collapsed for him, he was overtaken by "a calm but deep-seated recognition that this place was not just any place."[28]

Many people liken library usage to being transported to another place. Tzippy, a character in a novel by Tova Mirvis, exemplified this library-as-travel experience:

> Tzippy went back to the library every day, and the world around her widened. She pored over travel books. In the huge reading room silent except for the sound of pages turning, she saw the sculpted cathedrals of Tuscany, the canals of Venice, the chateaux of France. She took walking tours around Paris. She turned right at the Louvre and wished she could go inside and spend days there. She strolled through the Luxembourg Gardens. In coffee-table art books, she turned pages of water lilies and Degas dancers. She sucked in her breath at the beauty of light blue bows tied against feathery white ballet skirts.[29]

Death Remembered

Pilgrimages are often made to a spot where an individual or group death occurred. Impromptu roadside shrines are painful reminders at the sites of fatal accidents, attesting to the human need to mark such places. Within libraries, one hopes, no death is being memorialized—at least, none other than the deceased founders or donors whose names are engraved throughout.

Though library buildings may not specifically evoke the memory of an individual, the deaths of millions are being remembered there (see chapter 4). Beyond serving as a memorial, the library itself has been likened to a place of sacred remembrance. As early as 375 CE, one source saw the closing of a library as like the sealing of a tomb. Others have called libraries "granite-and-marble monuments."

Perhaps it is the association with death that makes the library seem a frightening place, which is how some library users—especially as children—report their library experience. When participants in a research project in

England were asked to recount their childhood memories of libraries, many remembered the library fondly. However, several respondents found the library scary—a "secret, forbidden" place, reported one. Another found it "beautiful, gloomy and mysterious." As Saul Bellow put it, "People can lose their lives in libraries. They ought to be warned."[30]

For others the library is not so much scary as intimidating. Library anxiety is the term used to describe the phenomenon of "an uncomfortable feeling . . . experienced in a library setting. Fear, feelings of uncertainty, and helplessness are all associated with the condition.[31] Some experience a feeling of shame at not knowing how to find library material. When addressing a gathering of librarians, a prominent member of a library board of trustees reminded her audience that just entering the library can evoke feelings of intimidation. The historical, elevated placement of the reference desk contributes to patron anxiety.

But others view libraries as safe spaces. In studying people's behavior in shopping malls, Paco Underhill discovered that feeling safe was one of the major attractions of shopping malls. Strolling down the aisle in the mall, "we are all in agreement about why we came here. . . . With that homogeneity of intention comes safety."[32]

CONTEMPORARY LIBRARY BUILDINGS

Much has been written lately about the library as place. Calling her President's Program "Coming Full Circle: The Library as Place," ALA president Carol Brey-Casiano noted that the library is a unique destination that will endure for generations to come. But library buildings of today and tomorrow must serve conflicting purposes. Not only must they offer both electronic and print resources; more profoundly, libraries must simultaneously provide public and private spaces.

Nostalgia remains for the grand reading rooms that inspired lofty thoughts and lowered voices, despite the fact that research has found that people now prefer small tables and human-size spaces in their libraries. In an interesting parallel, houses of worship are also now built to emphasize the communal aspects of the congregation rather than the ethereal, otherworldly aspects of the faith. Especially in what are called "seeker-sensitive" churches, buildings often look more secular than religious, mimicking malls with their large open spaces, flooded with light.

People no longer want to feel belittled—or quieted—by authority figures, be they librarians or ministers. Architectural changes have reflected this new approach. Contemporary libraries and many houses of worship have lowered their imperial platforms. Though libraries still use oversized counters and raised desks for reference stations, new library designs rarely elevate and separate the librarian station with iron rails. With the roving librarian concept some libraries try to eliminate the central station altogether.

Likewise, new houses of worship in many denominations have lowered the central dais from which the religious authority conducts services. One of the most contentious debates in my house of worship concerned the level of elevation of the pulpit. Some congregants went so far as to argue that there was no need to elevate the front at all, reflecting the congregation's outlook that rabbis are no higher than anyone else. Though most agreed philosophically, the front of the sanctuary was ultimately raised higher than the congregants so everyone could see—but the architect was mandated to elevate the area no higher than six inches.

Whether elevated six inches, six feet, or not at all, clergy and librarians still exert authority over their minions. Rarely, however, do they have the authority or inclination to maintain quiet in a library that is not designed for that purpose. As we see in chapter 7, libraries are—and arguably should be—the center for the community that supports it. Activities supporting social interactions among community members are vital and should be central for any successful library—yet community activities are rarely conducted in silence. Libraries of the future must find a way to accommodate both boisterous, lively interactions and quiet contemplation. Both are needed by those schizophrenic library users.

NOTES

1. Leckie, "Three Perspectives."
2. Lamott, *Plan B*, 143.
3. Rippel, "What Public Libraries Can Learn."
4. Underhill, *Call of the Mall*, 104.
5. "Thus Said . . . ," *American Libraries*, April 2005: 24.
6. As quoted in Kipnis, *Against Love*, 93.
7. As quoted in Griliches, *Library*, 39.
8. Pevsner, *History of Building Types*, 98.
9. The remainder of this section is drawn from Bostwick, *American Public Library*, 5; and Kaser, *Evolution*, 5–16, 47–60.
10. Klein, *Time to Be Born*, 212.
11. As quoted in Dowgiert, "Spirituality of Science."
12. Cahill, *How the Irish*, 133.

13. Palmer, *Hidden Wholeness*, 124; see also Palmer, *To Know*, 117–25, on the need for silence and solitude.
14. Palmer, *Hidden Wholeness*, 158.
15. Mandel, "Once Upon a Time."
16. Antin as quoted in Battles, *Library*, 198; Angle as quoted in Griliches, *Library*, 59.
17. Kaser, *Evolution*, 121, 122.
18. "Top 10 Annoying Library Noises in the U.K.," *American Libraries*, Oct. 2004: 21.
19. Isaacson, "Sanctuary in Libraries," 27.
20. Kaser, *Evolution*, 25.
21. Angle as quoted in Griliches, *Library*, vii; Antin as quoted in Battles, *Library*, 199; Griliches, *Library*, 59.
22. As quoted in Nathanson, *Over the Rainbow*, 405; see also Geertz, *Interpretation of Cultures*.
23. Cox, *Common Prayers*, 19.
24. Wolfe, *Transformation*, 14.
25. Mazur and McCarthy, *God in the Details*, 104; see also Pahl, *Shopping Malls*, 92.
26. Ostwalt, *Secular Steeples*, 142.
27. As quoted in Mazur and McCarthy, *God in the Details*, 104.
28. Cox, *Common Prayers*, 168.
29. Mirvis, *Outside World*, 191.
30. Pevsner, *History of Building Types*, 91; Black, "From the Outside In"; as quoted in Griliches, *Library*, 85.
31. Onwuegbuzie, Jiao, and Bostick, *Library Anxiety*, 29–30.
32. Underhill, *Call of the Mall*, 41.

CHAPTER SEVEN

Librarians and Libraries Promote Community

I recently discovered that a fellow librarian at work shares my passion for swimming. Since she swims almost daily, I asked if she had considered purchasing a home with a pool. "No, I don't want a private pool. I like the whole idea of a community pool instead of everyone having their own. I guess I'm just funny that way."

Without realizing it, her being "funny" about community swimming pools may be another expression of the main reason she chose the library profession. Librarians understand the benefits that derive from sharing resources rather than each one having his or her own. This preference for communal rather than individually owned resources is unusual in America's individualistic society.

Whether liberal or conservative, capitalist or communist, librarians know the limits of personal property. You cannot be an effective librarian cloistered away in your own library. Especially with the accelerating rate of information creation, no library will ever be self-sufficient. In a library, no matter how much you amass, it will never be enough. You have to share to gain access to the riches of the world's intellectual property.

NEED FOR AND SOURCES OF COMMUNITY

Although libraries are inherently community institutions, they are rarely recognized as such. When I told a friend about the premise of this book, it was the communal aspect of libraries that she asked me to explain. "Everything about a library promotes community," I told her. "Its very existence is the result of a community coming together to share resources. Think about borrowing a cup of sugar from the next-door neighbor. Isn't that an act that promotes and sustains a community? Libraries are the exemplary good neighbors. Their entire reason to exist is to enable neighborly sharing."

"I guess you're right," she said. "I never thought of it like that."

It was understandable that my friend would miss the subtle communal aspect of libraries. Checking out a book from a library appears to be a solitary activity. The person comes to the library alone, usually finds the book on her own, then checks it out to read alone.

But undergirding all of this apparent individual activity is the community at large. Societies with libraries—be they municipalities, colleges, or corporations—recognize the universal benefit of individual intellectual pursuits but acknowledge that no one person could or should own enough books to serve this purpose. And so the community comes together to purchase, store, and share the resources freely among its members.

Not only are the resources available to all, in our isolated society the library is also one of the few institutions that touch all. Whenever I would become upset by a student complaint about the library, a former boss would remind me: "On a college campus people complain about the cafeteria and library more than anything else. They are the only places *everyone* shares."

Despite the occasional complaint, people by and large like libraries and want them close at hand. Unlike the familiar "not-in-my-backyard" syndrome other institutions face, libraries are one of the top "desirable elements" people want in their residential areas, according to one major study. Only drugstores and food markets are more desired, and they nosed out libraries by just a fraction of a point (drugstores and food markets rate .91, libraries .89, on the "index of desirability"). Libraries garner higher desirability ratings than schools, community centers, churches, hospitals, or playgrounds. What is more, the library is one of the few places *all* population groups want. The elderly, households with children, without children, whites, blacks, Hispanics, upper income, lower income—everyone wants a library in their neighborhood.[1]

Along with libraries, other features home buyers want are coffee shops, Kinko's, and clubhouses, all areas that promote interaction among residents.

Sociability is so important that more people report wanting a friendly area than one safe or quiet.[2]

When all these features are put together, it appears that people long to create an atmosphere of community that has been lost. Columnist David Brooks notes that until recently people lived around some definable place they all shared: a tribal ring, an oasis, a river junction, a port. These were the geographic entities around which the community survived. But now in exurbia, each individual has his or her own polycentric nodes: the church, the subdevelopment, the office park.[3] Even schools, which used to be shared entities, often lose their universality when so many people opt for private alternatives to the neighborhood public school.

Not only do contemporary communities lack a shared geographic point, but residents are also growing farther apart. With the spread of gated communities and increasing home size, contact with one's neighbors grows ever rarer. Especially as people gain in wealth, their isolation increases. They purchase bigger and bigger homes separated from each other, resulting in lifeless neighborhoods that one critic said foster "segregation, isolation, compartmentalization, and sterilization."[4]

As one would expect, the isolation of residential housing has been accompanied by increasing feelings of loneliness and separation. According to Louis Harris polls, in 1966, 9 percent of people said they felt left out of things going on around them. By 1986 that number had grown to 37 percent. In 1966, 36 percent said, "What I think does not matter." In 1986 it was 60 percent.[5]

This increase in feelings of isolation has been attributed to a variety of causes. Andrew Solomon, an expert on depression, believes that spending a day watching television or a computer screen can contribute to feelings of isolation, noting that the rise in depression has accompanied increases in these activities.[6] Others think basic changes in society are to blame. Barry Schwartz, author of *Paradox of Choice*, observed:

> Our social fabric is no longer a birthright, but has become a series of deliberate and demanding choices. What was once given by neighborhood and work now must be achieved; people have to make their own friends . . . and actively cultivate their own family connections.[7]

Some blame the prevalence of today's celebrity culture for our estrangement. Sometimes we know more about the divorces, pregnancies, and intimate lives of Madonna or Britney Spears than we do about our neighbors.

Whatever the causes, many warn that dire consequences can result from chronic isolation. Sociologist Ray Oldenburg posits that, in the absence of a communal outlet, people's expectations toward work and family escalate beyond anything reasonable or possible. When the home and workplace fail to deliver sufficient succor—and usually they do fail because the need is too great—the resulting stress and strain can be disastrous. Oldenburg attributes the climbing divorce rate, absenteeism, and stress-related medical problems to lack of community. Something must be amiss, he notes, when the best-selling drugs in this country are tranquilizers and ulcer and hypertension medicine.[8]

On the other hand, connections with real people (not celebrity gazing) can evidently bring true happiness. Research has found that those who successfully weave social connections with others are rewarded with a sense of well-being that is lacking in loners. People who are married, have good friends, are close to their families, or participate in religious communities are happier than others.[9]

Communities are also vital to maintain what one historian called "a healthy social order." The founders of the U.S. Constitution included the right to free assembly as an antidote to tyranny. Totalitarian rulers ban informal gatherings to solidify their power. Residents of the former Soviet Union were fearful of talking freely in public. And lest we forget, as part of his successful reign of terror, Hitler banned assemblies of more than three persons on the streets of Germany.

Because contact with others is so vital to both human happiness and democracy, Americans turn to a variety of places where—as the *Cheers* television show put it—everyone knows your name. The most common places people look are discussed below.

The Third Place

The First Place is home. The Second Place is work. But the Third Place, according to Oldenburg, the term's originator, is where you head for "regular, voluntary, informal and happily anticipated gatherings beyond the realms of either home or work." In France the Third Place is the café, in Germany the beer garden, in England the pub. But no matter what the locale or location, all of these Third Places alleviate loneliness and foster the public good. In his foundational work, *The Great Good Place*, Oldenburg laments the lack of a Third Place in America. Though we nostalgically remember life in Mayberry, USA, sidling up to strangers at Denny's would be bizarre for most Americans. We don't even spend time talking to the people who live next door, let alone the person downing the Grand Slam Breakfast in the next booth. The teenager hamburger joints fondly remembered in *Happy Days* perhaps come as close to anything in America resembling a Third Place. But now these places, derogatorily referred to as "hangouts," evoke a more pejorative than desirable connotation. Arguably in America the neighborhood bar once filled this function, but no more. One telling statistic reveals the decline of these establishments: 90 percent of drinking in this country used to be done in public; now it is barely 30 percent.[10]

The national coffeehouse chain Starbucks was founded deliberately to create an Oldenburg-type Third Place. Major bookstore chains added eating and lounging areas for the same reason. Though these commercial entities have succeeded financially, none has been successful in creating the public discourse—or schmoozing, if you will—among patrons that is central to the idea of a communal Third Place.

Work as Community

For many Americans, work is where they find their community. Because we no longer exist in tight geographic communities, the body of water around which we gather is more likely the water fountain than the well. Or, as one social commentator noted, community ties have moved from the front porch to the water cooler. One survey found that two-thirds of all conversations among working adults take place at work, and another revealed that people get about 90 percent of their social connections from the workplace. Many studies have shown that having social connections with coworkers is the strongest single predictor of one's job satisfaction.[11]

The trend of finding fellowship through employment is well known among librarians. Anecdotal evidence suggests that a high percentage of librarians befriend each other, socialize together outside work, and marry each other. Membership in professional associations such as the ALA has increased 50 percent in the past two decades, perhaps as a result of the increasing attraction of socially gathering with colleagues.

Often in America work is expected to yield much more than a paycheck. Especially for those in professions such as librarianship, our "identity" is intertwined with what we do from nine to five. Indeed, some librarians approach retirement with trepidation, not only because they fear loosing their profession-based social community but because their identity is tied up with their work.

Work also provides a more illusive, profound aspect to our lives. "Identification" is too weak and modern a term for what we expect from our jobs. We also want to be subsumed by Something beyond us. We want to be not only invested but enmeshed in what we do. David Brooks noted that Americans have the unique ability "to slather endless amounts of missionary zeal on apparently trivial subjects and thereby transform them into harbingers of some larger transcendence."[12] This imagined Something we long for came before us, will be here after us, and explains the essence of who we are and why we are here. Work becomes the avenue of this immersion. Fortunately for librarians, the universal, transcendent aspects of libraries as discussed in this book are more apparent—and I would argue more real—than those of many places of employment.

Other Secular Communities

Beyond work, the secular venues to which people turn for community vary as widely as the people searching. Memberships in the local Democratic Party or the Flamingo Elementary School PTA provide an intimate sense of belonging, even bordering on the religious. "Sacred is the feeling that I belong here," explains community promoter Margaret J. Wheatley.[13] Any shared hobby— whether it be birding, bingo, or scrapbooking—can provide some of the essential elements of a Third Place. By bringing together people on a regular basis for conversation and companionship, these shared interests create a warm and welcoming environment for all.

Sports is one venue that can create community among a diverse gathering of people. Indeed, one critic noted that generalized loneliness gets covered up with "a wealth of frantic activity. That's the reason tennis has gotten so big. They all go out and play tennis."[14]

Like the world of work, sports can lend meaning to people's lives far beyond what appears on the surface. In some respects sports can even fulfill religious functions. Like religious gatherings, sports provide opportunities to achieve intimacy with real and imagined others. By wearing the colors of their team, sporting shirts emblazoned with logos and players' numbers, people can imagine themselves as part of the team. Baseball aficionados often bring gloves with them, hoping for the chance to participate in the game directly. With the emphasis on the character-building capacity of sportsmanship, sports can provide moral uplift. And the fervent loyalty fans express for their teams can be seen as nothing short of religious devotion. Sports is an excellent example of a secular community that resembles a religious congregation. So similar are these gatherings, scholars have difficulty defining the difference between them.

Religion and Community

When her child died, author Elaine Pagels sought and found comfort in the community of her church. As she put it, "Here was a place to weep without imposing tears upon a child; and here was a heterogeneous community that had gathered to sing, to celebrate . . . and to deal with what we cannot control or imagine."[15] Others seek this route for more mundane reasons. No matter what draws them, people seek out religious communities to fulfill their need for community—referred to in religious parlance as fellowship.

Though many people assume that a shared belief in a doctrine unites people of faith, it is the sense of community that serves as the attraction for many, if not most. As one Nazarene church member put it succinctly, "We agree with the doctrine, but the people are more important than doctrine."[16] Especially among young people, the congregation rather than doctrine attracts. They, like many of their elders, believe that answers to philosophical questions such as the meaning of life and ultimate purpose—if they exist at all—will come through a community of the faithful.[17]

The need for religious communion is especially pressing in a large, diverse, fragmented society such as America. When we can't agree on much, explain sociologists Michael Mazur and Kate McCarthy, religion provides shared acts of eating, dancing, and singing. "At least for a few moments, we can hold on to a slim thread of communal life."[18]

American Catholicism is famous for instilling communal loyalty among its members. Labor unions, political machines, government service—all communal organizations—have historically been encouraged and supported by Catholics.[19] Many Protestants convert to Catholicism because of its power to create community and overcome the isolation associated with American individualism.[20] "People pull" is also an attraction in Judaism. One study of ultraorthodox Jewish women found that a sense of belonging to an all-inclusive group was as important as, if not more important than, the search for tradition.[21] The study also revealed another important, though rarely acknowledged, religious attraction. Since many of them were single, the possibility of finding a suitable mate led many women to become orthodox. Whether they were returning to their religious roots or joining from nonorthodox or secular upbringings, many women became orthodox because orthodox men, it was rumored, make good husbands and fathers.[22]

LIBRARIES AS COMMUNAL SPACE

Religious institutions are far from the only places people go prospecting for potential mates. My husband remembers fondly using the public library for this purpose. "I used to go to the library to check out the babes, not the books," he says. My husband's choice of the library as the place to cruise chicks was no accident. Libraries are the central social gathering spot for many communities, colleges, and schools. Why else did the Internal Revenue Service select the library as its destination of choice for distributing tax forms? Libraries are the contemporary version of the communal well—the shared meeting spot for everyone in the community.

Because of this social-gathering-spot function, many a married couple trace their start to the library. Recently my own library was the site of a formal marriage proposal. The future groom got down on his knee in front of his beloved, who was studying in a carrel, and popped the question. If it were not for the shouts of approval by those studying in nearby carrels when she said "yes," no one ever would have known that the library had served as such a romantic location.

Though libraries do not often host marriage proposals, they do provide a safe, central place where everyone in the supporting organization feels welcome. Though libraries provide refuge from society (see chapter 6), they are also the center of it. On most college campuses the library is positioned in the center of the campus and referred to as the "heart" of the institution, geographically symbolizing the pursuit of knowledge as the focus of the enterprise. Library architect Henry Myerberg reminds us that school libraries provide "the biggest bang for the buck." Though they consume the equivalent of only two large classrooms, or about 5 percent of a school's real estate, libraries serve and inspire 100 percent of the school's teachers and students.[23]

Likewise, public libraries of old dominated their town squares, sitting proudly near other institutions representing permanence and trust: the courthouse, post office, bank. But more than any of these places, it was the library, along with the church (and it was usually *the* church in the singular), that was the physical and imagined center of a community. In libraries and houses of worship the group was recognized for being greater than its parts. Even the private acts of reading and praying were acknowledged to be more effective when done in the presence of others.

Community through Reading

Sharing books among people is obviously a communal activity. But so is reading. My editor and I vacillated over where a discussion on reading belonged in this book. Was it a solitary activity that should be discussed in the chapter on library as a place of solitude? Or was it communal? In truth, we decided, it is both. As psychologist Solomon noted, reading is neither a passive nor an isolating experience. "Reading is an entry into dialogue; a book can be a friend, talking not at you, but to you."[24] A homeless man interviewed in a shelter reported that the library was his destination of choice because there he could read and lose his loneliness in conversation with a stranger. "As long as I can read," claimed columnist Linda Weltner, "I am never alone."[25]

A community of readers may seem counterintuitive, but such a gathering fits perfectly into the contemporary definition of community. Perhaps because we lack a physical Third Place, as discussed above, in America communities are more imagined than real. As Brooks noted, "Our sense of belonging comes not so much from where the person believes they belong, but where they *want* to belong. The basis of community is what ideal state they aspire to." American communities come "from the person's head and heart rather than any place on earth."[26]

The community of all people reading the same book could be imagined as such a congregation of the like-minded. But beyond just being a time-spanning virtual community, the communal experience of reading also allows each individual to dissolve into Something larger, grander, greater, and longer lasting than herself. Indeed, when imagined thus, reading could be seen as a secular experience of the divine.

Communion with that greater Something is one way religion scholars refer to experiencing God. For many of us, falling in love most closely expresses this feeling of total absorption of the self. In the Bible, Paul spoke of such a feeling as God "in whom we live and move and have our being" (Acts 17:28). Harvey Cox describes this kind of divine feeling as being "not only around us but inside us, informing our senses and our feelings."[27]

According to Harold Bloom, romantic love, like reading, can be such an experience of the sublime. Though he admits that he is "not exactly an erotics-of-reading purveyor," Bloom believes that both reading and falling in love can be secular moments of transcendence. While acknowledging that people read for a variety of reasons—to come to know other people profoundly, to know ourselves better, for knowledge of self and others—for Bloom "the most authentic motive for deep reading . . . is the search for a difficult pleasure." Bloom urges readers "not to believe, not to accept, not to contradict, but to learn to share in that one nature that writes and reads."[28]

Communal Memory

Though experienced privately, reading is also an ongoing conversation between author and reader. Even death does not keep one from these communal conversations. Indeed, it could be argued that communicating from the grave is the main purpose of writing. Bloom noted that, though he turns to reading as a solitary praxis, he derives from it a sense of continuity with the past.[29] In singing the praises of the institution, Alfred Kazin noted that the entire idea of the library is to connect seamlessly with those who came before.[30]

The communal memory one taps in a library differs from history. History is the record of what happened, but communal memory is the experience of the narrative story as it was and as it will continue. For those from a strong ethnic or religious tradition, the group memory itself can become an object of reverence. It is not that the members of the group worship themselves; rather, it is the connection—the totality of the group's past, present, and future—that seems holy and immortal.

Religions use ritual and prayer to evoke this remembered tradition among the faithful. An effective prayer, notes Cox, is one that provokes a sense of holiness by linking a person to a tradition that goes back thousands of years. The worshipper senses a kinship with others around the world, as well as with those in previous centuries.[31]

In my own experience, performing a ritual preparation of a body for burial gave me the feeling of a direct link with my historical tradition. Washing the arm began my experience of time and space travel.

> I began wondering if someone had washed my *bubbe's* (grandmother's) arm like that. From *bubbe* my thoughts moved to her *bubbe*, and to her *bubbe*, and then to all the *bubbes* who have washed and been washed by Jewish women just like me. Suddenly, I was part of the permanence of the Jewish people who have performed this ritual for centuries.[32]

Library Communal Memory

For the secularly inclined, the religious milieu is not where an unending connection to previous generations is sought or found. Rather, the library embodies the union of past, present, and future. Libraries are imagined to include the history of anyone and everyone who ever managed to read or write a book. Beyond that, libraries also record the recording of history. Both the historical record of civilization and the history of the history can be found in the library. If God is imagined as Connection to History, library use becomes de facto worship. What else is library usage than the linking of a person with an ancient tradition? An eighth-grader reading a commentary on *Macbeth* may not imagine herself communing with the divine. Nor does an amateur gourmet consulting a cookbook for a recipe for cheese soufflé think he is performing a religious act. But both are linking themselves to a tradition. The student may simply be praying for a good grade, and the cook praying for a puffy dish, but they are also unknowingly praying to a secular library god.

SILENT AND SPOKEN LIBRARY COMMUNICATION

Beyond an ethereal sense of community, libraries also enable and encourage communication among those physically present in the building. Sometimes this communication is deliberate, but sometimes it is spontaneous and non-verbal.

Enormous amounts of information are transmitted over the carts of returned books. Without saying a word, members of a community exchange silent recommendations over the library version of the water cooler. What's good? What topics are hot these days? The racks of returned books speak volumes, if you will.

Before the days of automated circulation, the book pocket pasted to the back of the book would transmit the necessary secret information about good reads. Author Bel Kaufman remembers checking the card tucked inside as part of her selection process. "If the card was stamped with lots of dates, I knew I had a winner!"[33]

When talking is added to the process, the information exchanged can be better than any review in the *New York Times Review of Books*. "Was that any good?" asked of a patron returning a novel can provide a more direct and often accurate assessment than a hundred published book reviews.

Readers Advisory: A Community Effort?

The five words above that head this section are not mine. They are the title of an article published recently in *Public Libraries*.[34] The art of recommending titles to readers, known in the profession as readers advisory, remains a key element of librarianship. Learned through both formal classes and on-the-job training, librarians daily suggest books to their patrons. Of course, some librarians are better at this than others. But when a reader finds a librarian who manages to suggest just the right book, that advisor becomes a friend for life. When I was working at a public library, one day an elderly woman approached me, frantically asking, "Where's Mary? Where's Mary?"

"She's on break," I explained. "Can I help you?"

"No," she said emphatically. "I'll wait."

Responding to my quizzical look, she told me with combined desperation and affection, "I finished my book and I need Mary to tell me what to read now."

To aid librarians missing the skills of Mary, various online sources have been created that enhance and expand title recommendation. As the *Public Libraries* article discusses, these services have become "a virtual meeting place for books and readers." Many allow readers to both select the titles to be included and record their own impressions.

Amazon.com has become the resource of choice of many readers. By consulting this online information source, one can learn what the professional reviewing sources said of a title along with comments of readers much like those exchanged over the returned library books.

Book Discussion as Community

Some may argue that verbal and nonverbal exchanges about what to read next do not constitute a community, at least not in the classic sense of the word. Few, however, would take exception to characterizing a book discussion club as a community. According to one estimate, there may be as many as 30 million members in 750,000 special interest groups devoted to discussing books or current events or to pursuing shared interests.[35]

Libraries have a long history of encouraging and facilitating discussions about books. In the early days of American libraries, home libraries regularly deposited a few shelves of books into people's homes. Along with the physical books, a librarian was also dispatched to the home to engage readers in discussion. Book clubs with selected titles and discussion dates are now common features of many public libraries.

Thanks to Nancy Pearl and her One Book/One Community Program, communities grounded in books have expanded far beyond the confines of public libraries. The One Book concept began in 1998 when the Seattle Public Library and Washington Center for the Book introduced "If All Seattle Read the Same Book." Since then, similar book-based discussions have sprung up in cities, towns, communities, and organizations throughout the country.

Discussing books is a secular activity, but it forms the basis of many religious communities. Within Judaism not only are books sacred, but so is the discussion of their content. The weekly Jewish religious service features the ceremonial reading from the Torah. The Jewish tradition of discussing the Bible and its ancient commentary, the Talmud, is arguably the oldest continuous book club. By gathering to discuss these texts, many of which contain the varying points of view and opinions across generations, participants continue a seamless conversation over centuries.

Reading from holy texts also holds a central place in the worship service within Christianity and Islam. Bible study, which could be seen as the original One Book/One Community, is one of the fastest-growing programs in many churches, most likely because people are turning to this ancient source to seek relevance for their lives today. Religion scholars have noted a hunger for serious, soul-searching discussions of sacred texts within many denominations. Church leaders have been pleasantly surprised to find that participation in Bible study groups increases when the content becomes more rigorous. No longer satisfied to hear simply a recounting of the familiar Bible stories, congregants require discussions that plumb the meaning and history of the texts.

Whether discussing sacred or secular topics, communities that revolve around books and shared information create powerful assemblies. The University of Florida turned to communal reading when searching for a way to form esprit de corps and encourage racial dialogue among incoming freshmen. "Why Are All the Black Kids Sitting Together in the Cafeteria?" was the title chosen to encourage discussions of diversity and race. According to the program organizers, requiring all the students from diverse backgrounds to read and discuss the same book promoted community interaction. By literally getting them all on the same page, reading successfully provided participants an avenue to talk about their shared experiences.[36]

Community-Creating Library Programs

Libraries also promote community through library programs such as current events discussions, lectures, and films. Most major public library systems employ adult services staffs to organize and operate such programs. Even smaller public libraries manage to sponsor community events ranging from crafts demonstrations to spelling bees. Information and referral services, which identify major resources in a community and match individuals with them, have been a major activity of libraries for decades. According to one study, the provision of such community-based information was deemed more important by library users than reference service or popular reading materials.[37]

Library Architecture Reflects Community Function

In recognition of their community function, many libraries have been built with community rooms, lecture halls, and other spaces available for community groups. Even the activity of study, which was previously conducted by one person alone, has become a communal activity. "Study carrels are out; four-person tables are in," explains a building consultant. Likewise, students on college campuses are clamoring for group study space in their libraries because solitary reading assignments are often accompanied, or even replaced in some classes, by group projects. Since many libraries were not designed to support such activities, meeting this demand has been a challenge.

In many places, the library is the only facility with a publicly available community meeting room, so it becomes the de facto focal point for community-based activities by virtue of this physical facility. Public access computers are another physical feature that brings people to libraries and enhances the library role as a central gathering spot. Librarians sometimes lament that these computers are used only to check e-mail or play games, activities not thought of as traditional library use. If, however, building community is seen as a central role of the library, use of this communal shared resource fits perfectly into this mission.

Library Community-Building Programs

To find other ways to enhance their community building, librarians might investigate a new national initiative that helps libraries fill this role. The Libraries for the Future program, a division of Americans for Libraries Council (www .lff.org), helps libraries join foundations and community-based organizations to create and sustain community life. This national program currently operates three major programs to assist libraries.

1. Reading America, sponsored by the MetLife Foundation, provides training and technical support for libraries to use book and film discussions to foster intergenerational understanding and communication, especially in new immigrant families.
2. The Equal Access Libraries program, supported by the Bill and Melinda Gates Foundation, trains librarians to conduct needs assessment and create partnerships and public awareness programs that will strengthen their role as the community's center for information and learning.
3. The Family Place Libraries program strives to build healthy families and enhance literacy by creating spaces where young children and their caregivers can play and learn together.

LIBRARY VALUES THAT PROMOTE COMMUNITY

It is not by chance that libraries have taken the lead in many of the communal activities listed above. All libraries share the following values, which reinforce their role as community builders. Each of these values contributes to the library's central role as a communal institution that brings people together to share resources.

Publicly Available

From their beginning, libraries threw open their doors to everyone. The ancient library at Athens was *ad commenem delectationem*, "for the enjoyment of all."[38] Even the practice of chaining books to the shelves was done "for the good of the community." Modern-day reserve collections in academic libraries continue this practice; though no longer chained to the desk, certain books are put away and handed out selectively, to make sure these books remain available "for the enjoyment of all."

Libraries remaining open and making their riches accessible to all members of a community continues as a basic tenet of the library profession. The ALA Library Bill of Rights demands that books and library resources be provided "for all people of the community" and that library use not be denied or abridged because of origin, age, background, or views.

Because libraries are one of the few institutions that bring together individuals of all classes and castes, they have served as a great equalizer throughout history. Many have noted the diverse assemblage of human beings brought together in the public library. Nearly one hundred years ago one library user noted seeing in the library "everything from frumpery to finery." In the 1700s the library was described as an institution to which "the curious and impatient Enquirer . . . and the bewildered Ignorant might freely repair."[39] Alfred Kazin characterized the library as "an asylum and church of the unemployed."[40] Another public library user counted among the patronage "the unprocessed, misfits, left-overs, . . . hollow-cheeked, watery-eyed, shabby and furtively sad."[41]

Free

Rare in our consumer-based society, the library is open to all regardless of income. Everyone is invited to partake at no cost to the individual. Librarians sometimes forget just how remarkable this is. No other institution in American society exists for this purpose. Not even food—the very essential element for life—is provided in such a universal, free, all-you-want basis as books are in libraries. An immigrant from Venezuela, who later became a librarian himself, remembers his astonishment upon learning that the books in the library could be taken home for free. "I absolutely could not believe it when they told me that I could take a book—or lots of books—home. And that it would not cost me anything. In my country we didn't have anything like that!"

I remember my preschool daughter's confusion about this during one of our first trips to the library. Laden with an armload of picture books, she asked, "Where do we pay?"

"We don't, honey. It's free."

"Oh," she said and proceeded to the exit door.

"No, come back," I told her. "We do need to check them out."

"But I thought you said they were free."

Thus ensued a lengthy explanation on how checking out materials differed from purchase. An uncle of mine who spent his entire work life in the corporate world never grasped this concept. At family gatherings he would always ask me, "How's the library business?" Rather than engage him in a detailed discussion of how libraries are not commercial, I would just smile demurely and answer, "Just fine, thanks."

To the credit of those of us in the "library business," we have consistently insisted that the storehouse of knowledge residing within library walls—and on library computers—remains available free of charge to all within the community of users. User fees as a source of revenue for public libraries have been successfully opposed, even in those communities with residents who could easily afford them. Indeed, within American society, only the library and houses of worship are places one can go without expecting to pay anything (collection plates and overdue fines notwithstanding). Museums and parks may have "Free Fridays" or such, but these are often the exception rather than the rule. So extraordinary is this cost-free feature of libraries, one author deemed the free library movement one of the most important developments in the history of libraries.

Even those with substantial financial means still use the public library. While conducting research on the history of the Charleston library, one historian found that many families owned extensive private libraries but still frequented the public library. A modern-day example of the same phenomenon was demonstrated through a library bond issue. One wealthy woman announced her support of the campaign: "I never use libraries myself," she admitted, "but I want them available anyway." One fund-raising consultant noted that more often than not major donations to libraries come from people who do not even own a library card.

Though library resources are free, they can be priceless treasures. Harvey Cox has observed that human beings, especially those with money, can own and dispose of anything they choose. However, there never seems to be enough, because an overwhelming desire to purchase more and more overtakes them.[42] Unlike the emptiness created by tangible purchases, library usage can be deeply satisfying. Knowledge not only is free but can lead to priceless understanding. People may be infused with a desire to know more, which is rarely experienced as a hole to be filled.

Voluntary

The use of libraries—like religious attendance in this country—is voluntary, an important aspect for community formation. Except for students brought by teachers, no one is forced to use the library. Actually, library usage is frequently overreported, especially by teens who have been known to claim to be using the library while partying at the beach.

Self-selecting participation is an important feature of community formation. Tocqueville was especially taken with the vibrancy of the voluntary organizations he saw operating in this country, noting that these associations brought together diverse people in a way he did not witness in European countries.[43] David Brooks observed that Americans continue the tradition by creating their own social circles, each carrying its own status system, validation system, and role within society.[44] People find their place in the world within these chosen groupings.

Unlike families, which cannot be chosen, voluntary communities can be joined and left at will. Members must constantly affirm their affiliation to themselves and to others in order to justify their continued membership. Because no one is forcing anyone to remain, loyalty to the chosen community is high, which often translates into financial contributions. Just as Americans join more groups than any other nationality, they donate more money per capita than any other people. On average, American adults donate $1,100 per year to their voluntary organizations, with $3,600 given per year on average from evangelical Christians.[45] As mentioned earlier, libraries garner higher levels of community desirability than many other communal institutions. Therefore, the potential exists for libraries to capitalize on this loyalty through increased private donations (see chapter 9 for greater detail).

All Sides Welcome

Not only are all people invited to use the library, they are also free to explore any and all opinions there. "Libraries should provide materials and information presenting all points of view," proclaims Article II of the Library Bill of Rights. Nothing on the shelves of the library can be "proscribed or removed because of partisan or doctrinal disapproval." Intrinsic to the philosophy of libraries is the belief that no one has a monopoly on the truth. Wrestling with ideas is not only possible but encouraged. Sir Francis Bacon said that one should read "not to contradict and confute, nor to believe and take for granted, nor to find talk and discourse, but to weigh and consider."[46]

The emphasis on the library's free exchange of ideas may seem pedestrian to Americans, but it is exceptional in much of the world. A young woman from Latin America once told me that when she arrived in this country she found the teachers baffling.

> My teachers kept asking me, "What do *you* think?" "What do *you* think?" Whatever subject they were teaching, they all kept asking me what I thought. I would look at each one blankly. None of them understood. In my life before, in my country, no one had ever asked for my opinion on anything.

To guarantee that all opinions are exchanged freely, libraries value the protection of minority opinions and challenge attempts at censorship. Indeed, the academic world is based on and revolves around the free exchange of competing views. One author called academics' conferences and periodicals "out-loud challenges of one another's work."

Librarians steadfastly oppose efforts to suppress information and are loath to reveal the identity of those who have consulted their books and other materials. Likewise, librarians have vociferously fought efforts to employ Internet filtering software lest they inadvertently restrict access to information. "Conflict among books is what the universal library is about," says library historian Matthew Battles.[47] Librarians invite all members of their imagined community to come in and intellectually slug it out. Indeed, anyone who can read is invited into the intellectual free-for-all known as the library.

NOTES

1. Banerjee and Baer, *Beyond the Neighborhood Unit*, 134–39.
2. Brooks, *On Paradise Drive*, 50; Oldenburg, *Great Good Place*, 290.
3. Brooks, *On Paradise Drive*, 4.
4. Oldenburg, *Great Good Place*, 7, 285.
5. Schwartz, *Paradox of Choice*, 103.
6. Solomon, "Closing of the American Book."
7. Schwartz, *Paradox of Choice*, 110.
8. Oldenburg, *Great Good Place*, 10.

9. Schwartz, *Paradox of Choice*, 107.
10. Oldenburg, *Great Good Place*, 9.
11. Putnam, *Bowling Alone*, 85–90.
12. Brooks, *On Paradise Drive*, 193.
13. Wheatley, *Turning to One Another*, 133.
14. As quoted in Oldenburg, *Great Good Place*, 6.
15. Pagels, *Beyond Belief*, 4.
16. Wolfe, *Transformation*, 81–82.
17. Carroll and Roof, *Bridging Divided Worlds*, 83.
18. Mazur and McCarthy, *God in the Details*, 107.
19. Wolfe, *Transformation*, 263.
20. Porterfield, *Transformation of American Religion*, 62.
21. Wolfe, *Transformation*, 103.
22. Davidman, *Tradition in a Rootless World*.
23. Myerberg, "School Libraries," 12–13.
24. Solomon, "Closing of the American Book."
25. As quoted in Griliches, *Library*, 51.
26. Brooks, *On Paradise Drive*, 18.
27. Cox, *Common Prayers*, 21.
28. Bloom, *How to Read and Why*, 28–29.
29. Ibid., 22.
30. As quoted in Battles, *Library*, 203.
31. Cox, *Common Prayers*, 14.
32. Maxwell, "Final Touches," 54.
33. As quoted in Griliches, *Library*, 87.
34. Cohen, "Reader's Advisory."
35. Skocpol, *Diminished Democracy*, 170.
36. Peltz, "Faculty Assigned Summer Reading."
37. D'Elia and Rodger, "Public Opinion," 24.
38. Pevsner, *History of Building Types*, 91.
39. As quoted in ibid., 104.
40. As quoted in Battles, *Library*, 203.
41. As quoted in Black, "From the Outside In."
42. Cox, "Market as God."
43. As quoted in Putnam, *Bowling Alone*, 78.
44. Brooks, *On Paradise Drive*, 71.
45. Ibid., 77.
46. As quoted in Bloom, *How to Read and Why*, 22.
47. Battles, *Library*, 104.

CHAPTER EIGHT

Librarians and Libraries Transmit Culture to Future Generations

"*N*o, I won't give it to her," I insist. Despite the kind smile of the librarian behind the circulation desk and the stern instructions of my mother, I clutch the green book to my chest hoping Kiki, the red-headed girl pictured on the cover, will not be injured by my defiant action. After all, my adoration for this storybook character is the cause of my intransigence. Both librarian and mother reassure me I can find another Kiki book to take home, but I am as skeptical as any three-year-old can be.

"Please, Nancy. It's overdue," says my mother sternly.

I do not know what "overdue" means, but I know that my mother shakes her head and looks worried whenever she uses the word to describe Aunt Phyllis having a baby. To avoid evoking such a reaction, I reluctantly offer Kiki up to the librarian behind the counter. Though painful, my sense of loss is short-lived. Delight quickly takes its place when my mother says, "Let's go find another Kiki book."

Though I was only three years old, I obviously had already been indoctrinated into the library way of life. Just like religions, the library must infuse each new generation with its own mores, habits, and customs to sustain itself in the future. Inculcating children with faith—whether it be faith in the saving power of secular knowledge or a religious faith—is necessary for the continuation of any institution. Though the term "indoctrination" is sometimes pejorative—bringing to mind communist-style brainwashing—it is a necessary component of cultural transmission. Not only is the process essential, it is also extremely complicated. As religion scholar Diana Eck reminds us, civilizations, like religions, "are never finished products, packaged and ready to be passed from generation to generation." Rather, they are dynamic, changing; more like rivers than monuments.[1]

Libraries, like all institutions of culture, have their own unique ways of facilitating cultural transmission. A complicated mix of storytelling, rites of passage, and other rituals are needed to transfer the knowledge and wisdom of one generation to the next.

STORYTELLING

Tuesday at 10:00 a.m., many libraries across the country recount the narrative of their people. But unlike members of preliterate societies who gathered around the fire, in libraries preschoolers gather at the knee of the kindly children's librarian, who regales them with the parables of *The Cat in the Hat* and *The Runaway Bunny*.

Librarians sitting on child-size chairs slowly turning picture books before three- and four-year-olds may seem trivial, but it is anything but. Narrative stories are one of the most effective means of transmitting culture from one person to another. Many scholars, along with the general public, are growing skeptical about the ability of universal axioms or scientific theories to enlighten us. The pendulum is swinging in the other direction, with a belief growing that it is through stories that truth will be discovered.

Religions have long relied on storytelling as an essential element to reveal morality and transmit traditions. As Andrew Greeley puts it, "Religious heritages constitute story-telling communities."[2] Each religion is a "contest of narratives," says Bill Moyers, each with multiple meanings.[3] Often the listener is blithely unaware of the underlying messages of these tales. Children especially are amused by stories without realizing that subtle learning is taking place. Whenever my daughter returned from Sunday school, I would ask her, "What did you learn in school today?" She would usually respond, "Nothing. Rabbi Sarah just told us some stories."

What appeared to her as "just stories" is now believed by many religion scholars to be an essential part—if not the most important component—of a religion. Indeed, the basis of many religious traditions can be found by examining their stories of ordeals, death, and resurrection.[4]

Everyone from child psychologist Bruno Bettelheim to best-selling author Stephen King has noted the powerful punch of the fairy tale. Something about these stories compels their retelling over and over. No matter how many times we hear them, they continue to fascinate.

Business experts are even finding that stories can help improve the bottom line. Stories that look forward, known in business parlance as scenarios, have become important forecasting tools for organizations. As two consultants explain, "Stories that paint a vivid picture of a future state can help provide vision and leadership. . . . PowerPoint slides often do not do a good job of communication because they lack contextual meaning. Stories, on the other hand, relate context."[5]

Along with library story time, other forms of cultural transmission can be found within the library building. Many libraries sponsor intergenerational programs that rekindle this ancient rite of passing experiences from one generation to the next. Especially effective are programs that bring teens together with Holocaust survivors or World War II veterans. Beyond just "telling stories," these intimate exchanges transmit the experiences of a person, along with that of an entire time and culture.

Storytelling narratives are by no means limited to children. Librarianship tells itself a story about the centrality of this profession to civilization; indeed, this book could be counted among this narrative stream. But we are not alone. It has been said that every profession has its story that must be believed at some level by those claiming membership within the group.[6]

RITUALS

Storytelling is but one of many avenues cultures use to transmit tradition. Defining exactly what constitutes a ritual, like defining religion, is difficult and the center of long-standing debates. Sometimes rituals are formal and required, but often they are informal and hardly recognized for the importance they carry. Some argue that the informal method is most effective. Andrew Greeley believes that much of the Christian heritage is transmitted to the very young at Christmastime, and that Jewish children receive their major heritage lesson at the Passover seder. Indeed, he conjectures, "After both events the child has learned everything that is important to belong to the heritage."[7]

Rituals can provide a sense of community by bringing isolated individuals together toward a common goal and providing them the opportunity to achieve intimacy with real and imaginary others. Reassuring us that we all see the world in the same way, rituals help resolve conflicts that can threaten collective life.

Most of us use rituals to ensure a positive outcome or ward off a potential threat. "It is as if the repeated words, the predictable action and the familiarity of the ritual acts offer a safe and comfortable route through crisis situations."[8] Rituals help us maintain control, or think we have managed such a feat. As we try to make sense of our at-times apparently senseless, chaotic lives, rituals bring us order and meaning.

Library Rituals

At first blush, this litany of ritual elements may seem remote from the library world. But much of the routine activity seen in libraries fits the definition and benefits derived from ritual enactment.

A friend of mine would take her five-year-old son to the neighborhood library every week. One day she and her son were on the other side of town to do several errands. Since she knew of a branch library in this vicinity, she told him, "When we finish with the bank, we'll go to the library." True to her word, she proceeded to the library as soon as she had finished using the ATM. "We're here," she announced as she parked in front of the library. To her amazement, her son immediately started crying. "What's the matter?" she asked. All she could make out amid his sobs were the words "pink library, pink library." When he had calmed down a bit, he explained, "I want to go to the pink library. You said we were going to the library. My library is pink, not green." As she studied the green painted wall before her, she realized that the facade of their usual library branch was pink. More important, she understood the comfort her son took from going to the same place and following the same routine in his library usage.

Changing library location was traumatic for this five-year-old, but it can also be disorienting for those fifteen or fifty. As anyone who has ever been involved in closing or moving a library is well aware, powerful emotions are associated with libraries. Librarians sometimes lose sight of the fact that library usage is a daily occurrence for an astounding number of people. One of the most surprising results of a user study at my own community college library was that 37.7 percent of people said they were in the library every day.[9]

Any activity done so routinely is bound to become ritualized. As they do in church, people often sit in the same place in the library. They read the same paper or magazine. They say hello, or at least nod or smile, to the same staff members. Many of these actions can become mini-rituals, deeply engrained and profoundly troubling if forced to be changed or abandoned.

Library Rites of Passage

The rite of passage, marking a child's passage from childhood to adulthood, is one of the most basic cultural rituals. Anthropologist Victor Turner notes that these types of rituals can be transformative and powerful because of their capacity to move an individual from one social status to another.[10] Rites of passage indicate that the novitiate has moved through various stages, which Paco Underhill saw demonstrated when he watched teens buying jeans at the mall. "You go from being ignorant to being somewhat knowledgeable to being a member of the club, which imparts a cult-like status."[11] Confirmation and the bar and bat mitzvah are examples of religious rites of indoctrination.

Libraries have their own required rite of passage. Rather than slaying lions or delivering a bat mitzvah speech, library neophytes must perform a literate society's most basic skill—the writing of one's name—in order to gain access to the adult world of communal knowledge. Once this ability has been demonstrated, the library confers upon children their keys to the adult world in the form of their first library cards. The bestowal of this first library card can be seen as what Greeley called a small, quiet, almost private ceremony, barely acknowledged publicly but inwardly astounding.[12]

I remember distinctly the conferral of my first library card. After laboriously engraving my name on a library application, filling two-thirds of the form with the letters NAN, I presented my handiwork to the librarian. She studied the card dramatically, then smiled and pronounced, "That's a very good job, Nancy. Let me type your card." Disappearing behind a black machine that smelled of oil and ink, she reappeared several minutes later clutching an orange tagboard paper just the size of my hand. "This is a very important card," she said handing it to me. "Don't lose it."

I knew I would never lose it, but I did not know at the time that I had just participated in one of the most important rituals of a literate society. Indeed, many famous writers recognize how gaining access to the riches of the library altered their lives. Peter Hamill claims, "The library is a place where most of the things I came to value as an adult had their beginnings." Author Rita Mae Brown says her life began when she received her first library card. Jerzy Kosinski credits the public library with being the one place he could find out who he was and what he was going to become. For Jean Fritz discovering libraries was like having Christmas every day.[13]

To heighten the drama of the act, one library lets children write their name in "The Book," an impressive ledger, when they are granted their first library card. Here is a permanent record displaying all those who are now able to perform this valuable feat.

Libraries and Independence and Maturation

Libraries also represent one of the first steps of a child toward independence from home and hearth. Lions, which represent independence, are often associated with libraries. The famous lions guarding the New York Public Library, Patience and Fortitude, were strategically placed above eye level to impart "a feeling of independence yet rendering the friendly air of a pussy cat rather than ferocious beast."[14]

The library, like the church, is one of the first destinations children are allowed to venture without adult supervision. In recent years the shopping mall has been added to the list, in some cases replacing the other two. But for many generations, attending church or going to the library was one's first taste of independence. Harvey Cox remembers fondly that, because his parents were not churchgoers, he delighted in the opportunity to break from the tight family circle and participate in the adult world by attending Sunday morning services alone.

This sense of liberty was captured by Tzippy, a character in Tova Mirvis's novel *Outside World*, who reminisced about being a child in the library, where

> she felt flush with the freedom that she could do whatever she wanted as she wandered the aisles of books. The library was huge, filled with cavernous spaces where she could wander. She wanted to read her way through the building. She wanted to consume everything in sight.[15]

In a major research project in which adults were asked to recall their childhood experiences, they repeatedly related the sense of liberation, maturation, and awe that libraries provided them as youngsters. "I remember the joy of moving from the Junior to the Senior library," said one. Much like attaining a driver's license, gaining access to the "adult" section of the library both officially sanctioned that they had reached an important milestone and allowed for unlimited access to new worlds.

One of the most important lessons cultures must transmit to the next generation is sexual information. Libraries have long contributed to sexual education of the young. Countless individuals—famous and not-so-famous—credit the library as being their initial source of sexual information, and sometimes even being the site of their first sexual experience. Roger Straus II, the son of the publishing house Farrar, Straus and Giroux, remembers having what he called his first "literary orgasm" at age fourteen.[16] Others recount seeing their first naked breast in the *National Geographic* or learning the meaning of slang words for body parts in *Webster's Unabridged Dictionary*.

Perhaps it is no coincidence that most censorship issues arise from reading materials for two age groups: children from four to six and from fourteen to sixteen years of age.[17] In both of these age ranges, children are taking major steps toward independence. The younger group is learning to read on their own. The older children are beginning to go places unaccompanied for the first time. In both cases, their parents may prefer to limit this newfound freedom and keep them protected from the perceived dangers by limiting their reading material.

As one would expect, the first experience of independence frequently leads to the misuse of the privilege. Children's librarians are well aware that otherwise perfectly behaved children sometimes act up when given the opportunity in a library. Sunday school teachers have also observed the phenomenon of "good kids" being bad in church when released from the scrutiny of their parents.

A century ago the misdeeds of children were not so much observed in their library behavior as in their reading habits. The librarian's role, as library historian Matthew Battles recounts, was to entice young readers into the children's room to begin the process of guiding them to right reading.[18] A major figure in library history, William Frederick Poole, counseled his fellow librarians to treat children with understanding:

> Often in youth people would read novels excessively. Every person goes through a limited period when he craves novel-reading; and perhaps reads novels to excess. However they often pass safely out into broader fields of study, and this craving never returns.[19]

Children's and Young Adult Spaces and Programs

Though Poole urged compassion, libraries have not always been warm and welcoming to children. According to library historian Arthur Bostwick, before 1890 there existed practically no systematic effort to provide library facilities for children.[20] If it were not for the introduction of open shelving, libraries may have remained off-limits to children. When libraries were closed stacks, patrons were required to submit requests for books that were retrieved from storage. Those few children's books owned by libraries were shelved with the other books and delivered to children who had submitted the required call slips. When the stacks were opened to patrons, many libraries maintained the accession number order that had been in use in the closed stack arrangement.

In no time, however, it was determined that the children were interfering with adult users. Complaints led to removing all children's fiction books from the adult shelves and making a children's corner where young readers could be kept more or less by themselves. Many libraries maintained the accession number shelving system for children's nonfiction because it would not only spare librarians the burden of reclassifying all the books but was also hoped to "surreptitiously uplift children's reading habits as they would be more likely to select non-fiction." However, even this arrangement proved to be problematic, and soon children were provided their own separate room, and ultimately their own library.[21]

Contemporary children's and young adult services continue to provide both the reading material and physical space youngsters need to explore the library world, and by extension the world itself, independently. Whether it be a separate children's room, alcove, or section, libraries must provide a safe environment for exploration. However configured, children's sections must be friendly without being childish. Library architect Henry Myerberg notes that with the proper use of scale, materials, and color, the library can appear both sophisticated and whimsical while not looking like an amusement park.[22] The goal of children's library design is to create an exciting place where children have fun learning.

While children are enjoying their library area, the adults accompanying them may have their own form of fun. As discussed in chapter 7, the library is one of the few places in a community that brings people together. The national Family Place Initiative facilitates interaction among adult caregivers. The aim of this and other such programs is to create a self-help network for parents. One researcher studying such a caregiver gathering was taken aback by the "noise, bustle, and sometimes confusion" that reigned; but, most important, displays of informal support and mutual enjoyments were evident.[23]

Teen sections of libraries mimic their patrons' station in the world: beyond the bounds of the children's section but not yet totally integrated into the adult world. Many library teen areas create an inviting space for young adults to gather, read, or—to borrow one of their own phrases—"just chill." "We wanted the library to become the "it place," explains youth services librarian Kati Tvaruzka in an article section aptly titled "How We Get Them Here and Keep Them Comfortable."[24]

The Louisville Free Public Library went beyond the standard teen area and created a teen branch adjacent to the main facility. Actually, it was the teens themselves who designed the collection, furniture, and programming. So different is the resulting library that most adult passersby who enter want to know, "What is this place?" One person learning it was a library responded, "We never had anything like this when I was growing up, but I think it's wonderful. Teens need someplace like this."[25]

Libraries that have not gone so far as to create a teen library still offer a variety of programs and services to facilitate their library exploration and fun. Books clubs, writers clubs, poetry slams, film showings, and contests are among the activities offered by library children's and young adult departments. One library even sponsored a "lock-in" for young adults after the library closed, where assuredly there were plenty of stories read.

Card Catalog as Ritual

Those of a certain age may remember that one of the first challenges to mastering the use of the library was the card catalog. Leaning on the wooden counters of the library shrine, flipping through those 3- by 5-inch cards gave one a sense of mastery and empowerment. When the required card was found, like Jews at the Wailing Wall, the numerical desire would be jotted down on a piece of scrap paper. Rather than leave our prayers, we would clutch those slips and head to the stacks, praying that our scribbled code would be found on the shelf.

But leave it we must, for libraries no longer offer patrons this temple of wooden drawers, having replaced it with an insistent blinking cursor on a computer screen. Though this system is eminently more efficient, many people lament the loss of their beloved card catalog, much as pre–Vatican II Catholics miss the sound of the Latin Mass. Indeed, the extreme resistance to the discontinuation of the card catalog suggests that it meant more to people than simply a library index. The practice of using the card catalog—at least aspects of how people interacted before the shelves—could be interpreted as a ritual.

This ritual has now been replaced with a computer system that is both wonderful and terrifying—wonderful for its ability to search instantly and bring the entire world of information within milliseconds. But this ability is terrifying as well, for that incessant blink demands that you know the magic words. The machine stands ready to fulfill your every need and desire much like a genie, but you must provide the correct incantation to send it on its way. Somehow, the cursor intimidates and humiliates. The computer forces the searcher to admit he or she does not know the secret passwords.

No wonder library users experience guilt in libraries and confess their ignorance to librarians. Few of us—dare I say librarians included—know exactly what we want and how to retrieve it. But the blank screen humiliates by somehow assuming we should.

Compare this sense of shame and guilt wrought by the computer with the emotions evoked by a card catalog. Like electronic searching, the card catalog also required instruction in its use. It awaited our approach like a computer screen, but mastery seemed possible, even an intellectual point of pride. Those of us old enough to have received training in card catalog use as children may remember it as a rite of passage. Once we learned to decode the numbers and order of the cards, we felt we had dominion over the world of knowledge.

One of the most important aspects of the ritual of card catalog use was its ability to convey a systemized order. Especially important in this chaotic time, rituals offer the appearance of order. Beyond that, however, the card catalog inspired feelings not just of control but of intimate familiarity and mastery. Historian Barbara Tuchman said, "For me the card catalogue has been a companion all my working life. To leave it is like leaving the house one was brought up in."[26] One library even staged a mock funeral when it initiated a new automated library information system.

Books as Ritual Items

Along with learning how to access the library, children also must be taught to respect the institution and its resources. Central to that education is learning respect for the physical object of the book. Books can carry meaning beyond their form and shape. The book can serve as an icon—a sign or representation of a sacred personage or being. The holy to which a book points is not a person or a god or God; rather, it represents knowledge and truth.

At least I know that books fulfill this purpose for me. I am agitated by the sight of books being thrown away and delighted by the sight of a child reading one. The physical book is not simply a mundane object to me. In attacking an article I wrote on library technology,[27] one critic called me "a bibliofundamentalist." I wear that epithet with pride, for my feelings about books do border on the religious.

My Jewish upbringing probably influenced my feeling about books. In some Jewish denominations it is customary to kiss the prayer book at the conclusion of the religious service. As a child in religious school, I was taught that any book containing the name of God that dropped to the floor should immediately be kissed the way one would kiss a child who had fallen.

But it is not only Judaism that treats books as holy objects. The Bible serves as an icon in many religious denominations, employed during the service as a symbol of a path to divinity, if not to the divine itself. Church historian Martin Mary noted that in the United States by the 1800s the Bible had become an icon in mind, home, church, and culture.[28] Librarians, library users, and book lovers have expanded this icon from The Book to Books as sacred objects.

It is incumbent upon children's librarians to impart this feeling of awe and wonder for books to children. Librarians sometimes underestimate just how important this role is. According to one study, most people believe it more important for the public library to serve as children's door to learning than to serve as a research center, community center, or provider of reference service.[29]

Though electronic information surrounds children today from their preschool years on, books will still be central in imparting the written record of civilization. Sitting cross-legged on the floor at story time, children are read to from a book. When they are tucked in at bedtime, Mom reads to them from a book. When they are ready to learn what are euphemistically called the facts of life, they do so from a book. As they grow older, just about anything they want to know can be found through a book. As the Bible puts it, there is truly nothing new under the sun. Because some writer took the time to think it and commit it to paper, and some librarian found it, cataloged it, and preserved it, that piece of knowledge stands awaiting discovery by future generations. Once they have made it through their rite of passage, all that knowledge is theirs to discover on the shelves of a library.

NOTES

1. Eck, *New Religious America*, 9.
2. Greeley, *Religion as Poetry*, 42.
3. Moyers, *Moyers on America*, 48.
4. Nathanson, *Over the Rainbow*, 250; see also Cox, *When Jesus*, on the importance of stories.
5. Neilson and Stouffer, "Narrating the Vision," 26.
6. Molotch, *Where Stuff Comes From*, 24.
7. Greeley, *Religion as Poetry*, 46.
8. Mazur and McCarthy, *God in the Details*, 106.
9. Miami-Dade Community College North Campus Student Survey, November 2002.
10. As discussed in Mazur and McCarthy, *God in the Details*, 105.
11. Underhill, *Call of the Mall*, 83.
12. Greeley, *Religion as Poetry*, 47.

13. As quoted in Griliches, *Library*, 67, 29, 119, 73.
14. Milton, "Urban Lions Fortitude."
15. Mirvis, *Outside World*, 190.
16. As quoted in Lerner, *Forest for the Trees*, 189.
17. LaRue, "Buddha at the Gate."
18. Battles, *Library*, 198.
19. As quoted in ibid., 148.
20. Bostwick, *American Public Library*, 87.
21. Ibid., 89, 195–96.
22. Myerberg, "School Libraries," 11.
23. As quoted in Oldenburg, *Great Good Place*, 237.
24. Tvaruzka, "Teen Lounge."
25. Saunders, " Young Adult OutPost," 116.
26. As quoted in Griliches, *Library*, 57.
27. Maxwell, "Seven Deadly Sins."
28. As described in Prothero, *American Jesus*, 80.
29. D'Elia and Rodger, "Public Opinion," 24.

CHAPTER NINE

Implications of Libraries as Sacred, Secular Institutions

There is nothing in our cultural armory more important than the library . . . nothing. If every school, every university, every other source of knowledge were destroyed, but the library survived, civilization could be rebuilt.

—Harrison Salisbury

ecause my husband and I are both librarians, my teenage daughter is often asked if she plans to pursue a career in librarianship. Like so many kids her age, she laughs at the idea. But awe, rather than guffaws, would be a more appropriate reaction to the possibility of joining the ranks of the library profession. As I argue throughout this book, librarians—though working in secular institutions—fulfill a higher purpose in people's lives. People lose themselves and find their souls in libraries. Librarianship is nearly a sacred calling.

It is understandable that a teenager would not recognize the essential nature of the profession or institution. Unfortunately, many librarians also underestimate the devotion that draws them to the profession and the profound effect they have on people's lives. Howard F. McGinn, dean of university libraries at Seton Hall University, admits that he was totally unprepared for one discovery he made while researching minority librarian job satisfaction: "Black librarians felt librarianship as a calling and that they were doing the work of God. It was really striking."[1]

But it is not only black librarians who describe their career choice in religious terms. A similar religious zeal draws librarians of all racial, religious, and ethnic persuasions to the field. Though many librarians experience librarianship as a personal calling, few realize how widespread this feeling is among the profession.

Likewise, librarians fail to comprehend the vital necessity of their institution to people's lives. "I cannot live without books," said Thomas Jefferson. Many library users would agree. They cannot live without books or libraries. Consider what would happen if, as posed in the epigraph of this chapter, "every other source of knowledge were destroyed, but the library survived."[2] Civilization would be rebuilt thanks to the preserved knowledge on the library shelves. Librarians must remind themselves of the indispensability of their profession and institution.

LIBRARIANS MUST SPEAK OUT

Beyond simply recognizing their importance and feeling good about themselves and their profession, it is incumbent upon librarians to act on this knowledge. If librarians believe—rightly, in my opinion—that their institution can save individuals, communities, and society at large, they have a responsibility to speak out.

Historically, librarians have been excellent service providers but not such great self-promoters. "The truth is," said two library educators, "librarians have failed to explain to those outside the field what contributions they and their institutions actually make to society at large." "Those of us who have committed our life's work to the improvement of libraries are continually frustrated with our lack of ability to effectively 'tell the library story,'" said Peggy Rudd, director of the Texas State Library and Archives Commission."[3] "Librarians need to learn how to speak out," observed one library advocate and trustee.[4]

Now, more than ever, the continuation of the institution of the library depends on them speaking out. Many people have come to question the need for libraries, thinking that online information does the library's job, only better. Librarians must quickly learn how to insert themselves forcefully into public policy discussions and correct this misconception.

Librarians who defend the institution of the library will find that they make forceful advocates for their cause. Librarians are highly respected and esteemed members of the community. Like the old E. F. Hutton commercials, when librarians speak, people listen. So respected are librarians, they sometimes cause anxiety to those in their presence. A guest speaker at a library conference confessed to me that she was comfortable speaking to all types of people except librarians. "I get so intimidated by librarians in the audience. I mean, what can I possibly tell them that they can't look up themselves?"

Librarians are awarded public respect and trust because in many ways they function as priests, ministers, and even gods. Like ancient priests, librarians seem to possess secret incantations that make things materialize out of thin air. When they type secret words into a computer, suddenly the requested book, article, date, or name appears as if by magic. Librarians lose sight of the fact that no other profession can do this. We alone are consulted no matter what the question or problem. Though subject specialists may know more about their field of interest, librarians remain the high priests of knowledge. "Intellectual physicians" is an apt description of our profession, but, unlike our medical counterparts, librarians are generalists. Just like ancient holy priests, librarians know all.

Librarians are also like ministers, missionaries of the mind pointing the way to intellectual salvation. "READ" posters, library instruction, information literacy, teen advisory groups, tutoring assistance are just a few of the secular strategies librarians employ to help users help themselves. Now that "spiritual, not religious" has replaced traditional religion for so many, the library is a natural place to turn when searching for life's meaning and purpose. Especially for highly educated, institution-distrusting baby boomers, the quest for answers to the ultimate questions in life leads directly to libraries and librarians.

In some aspects, the role of the librarian could even be seen as holy. The most popular notion of God today is the "flashlight God," gently illuminating the path to a better life. Librarians, like God, guide people to their ultimate destinations and internal truths. Librarians serve as intermediaries to this type of God, holding aloft the flashlight of wisdom.

LIBRARIANS MUST DEMAND LIBRARIES AS SPIRITUAL, SACRED SPACE

When these respected and revered librarians raise up their voices, the first topic they should speak about is the need for the physical library building. Just a few years ago everyone was talking about the library as an obsolete institution, soon to be replaced by the Internet. In the late 1990s, some college and university administrators openly questioned the future of the campus library.[5] Library bond issues failed and some municipal libraries even closed their doors, such as the highly publicized Salinas, California, library. But, to paraphrase Mark Twain, rumors of the library's demise have been greatly exaggerated.

I am convinced that the library as a physical entity will remain—not only because print is here to stay (discussed below) but because of the powerful emotional pull of the library. Indeed, there is a spiritual quality to the use of the library that is real, though grossly underappreciated.

Many library users go to the library building for quiet contemplation and study, much as they would go to church. Too often librarians and architects forget the nearly religious quality of the grand old library, with massive reading rooms where "voices are lowered and minds raised." "Reading," said Proust, "is on the threshold of the spiritual life."[6] The library, like a house of worship, is a public location one seeks when grappling with private thoughts. Whether one comes to pray or to read, somehow one's inward search is enhanced by the presence of others likewise engaged. No words need be exchanged—indeed, silence is one of the major attractions of the place—yet knowing others are also seeking is comforting.

"Sanctuary" is a religious term, but one often used in conjunction with library space. An author I know travels across the country speaking about his books. "To compose myself and gather my thoughts before each speech, I find the nearest library," he said. "I sit quietly there for a few minutes. No matter where I am, just being in a library calms me."

LIBRARIANS MUST REMEMBER SPIRITUALITY OF BOOKS

As a getting-to-know-you exercise at a recent meeting at work, attendees were asked to recount a childhood experience that exerted an effect on them throughout life. An astounding number of them recounted memories involving reading. Retreating to a treehouse to read, sneaking peaks at what was then the scandalous novel *Lolita*, snuggling into Grampa's lap as he read. The remembrances were powerful and carried much more significance than simply nostalgic moments. As Sen. Barack Obama recounted dramatically in his keynote address at the ALA Conference in 2005, "Every one of you can probably remember the look on a child's face after finishing their first book."[7]

For some people library usage is remembered as a rite of passage, bestowing a sense of mastery and independence. Successfully writing one's name for the first time and receiving a library card granted admission to the adult world of the written word. Many used this newfound freedom to learn about sex.

Perhaps because they work with them every day, librarians sometimes lose sight of the impact that a room filled with books can make. There is something magical about the physical object of the book. "People seem to want to see books and be near books," concluded one librarian after several library building projects had to be redesigned to accommodate this desire. "Even if they don't use the books, people want to be around them."

Being in the presence of books not only allows for those wonderful serendipitous finds but evokes a powerful emotional response, bordering on a religious feeling. Books themselves carry a quasi-religious quality. Nancy Pearl said, "Books allowed me to both find myself and loose myself in them."[8] Perhaps nowhere is this more obvious than in the recent scandal over the alleged desecration of the Koran by U.S. interrogators. Fifteen people died and scores were injured as a direct result of the symbolic power of the book.

The emotional appeal of books can be a double-edged sword for librarians. Additional support for library space and materials can be garnered because people want to have books at hand. Because of this reverence for the physical item of the book, however, disposing of unneeded materials can be tricky. Perhaps because books represent the thoughts of a living person, both the public and librarians are aghast at the sight of books being thrown away or destroyed. Yet given their limited space, libraries must withdraw items continually.

One way out of this problem would be for librarians to design a better system of recycling unneeded books. Current exchange programs exist, but they rely heavily on listing titles available, in the hopes that someone can use them. Though useful, these programs meet with limited success. I have often fantasized about a regional used-book depository that would give away or sell all unneeded library books. Not only would it provide a little money for the participating libraries, more important, it would find a loving home for books much like an animal shelter locates loving places for pets. Such a program would both encourage the reverence people feel for books and free up valuable library space for new books to take their place.

LIBRARIANS MUST DEMAND SPACE FOR BOOKS

As long as books remain in physical form, space will be needed to house them. When coupled with the powerful, nearly religious pull of the library space, librarians can make a powerful case for new library buildings, or at least the provision of adequate shelf space in current buildings. Clifford Lynch reminds us that the prediction that books will be replaced has been just around the corner for fifteen years. In fact, predictions of the impending doom of libraries have a long history. In the early 1980s, when compact discs efficiently stored and retrieved information then available only on paper, many thought the paper-based library was finished. When *Time* magazine chose a computer as "man of the year" in 1982, many feared the end of libraries was nigh, with technology replacing "the old library-centered cosmology."[9]

Librarians of a certain age may remember when the advent of microfilm threatened to replace library buildings with shoe boxes. This fear lasted only for as long as it took to realize the difficulty of using this new technology. As was soon realized, microfilm machines make people dizzy, are difficult to use, and constantly break down. (I challenge you to find a library that does not have at least one broken microfilm reader taking up space at this moment.)

Despite the inaccuracy of these microfilm projections, arguments that technology will replace libraries still persist. To some, primarily those who see themselves as technologists/information scientists, the future of libraries resides solely in purveying online information. In this automated utopia, computers search and retrieve anything and everything that anyone could ever need or want, on demand, instantaneously, with nary a piece of paper in sight.[10] Lending credence to this vision of the obsolete library was a faculty member who proudly reported that in fifteen years he had to come to the library only once, and that was to get one old book. In this dire vision of their future, libraries become simply managed study halls and online websites, with digitized books replacing paper copies and negating the need for the library as physical space.

Others have warned that librarians supporting such a future are intoxicated by the power and abundance of technology, having lost sight of the fact that they must offer service, not simply access.[11] ALA president Michael Gorman suggests dampening the "fanfare and hoopla" surrounding the massive book digitization project announced by Google. "Digitized whole books are expensive exercises in futility based on the staggering notion that, for the first time in history, one form of communication (electronic) will supplant and obliterate all previous forms."[12]

Books will remain in physical format because they remain remarkably useful and effective. Librarians should rejoice—and extensively publicize several studies that show that access to books, trips to libraries, and simply possessing a library card have all been associated with children's higher test scores and improved reading. When students have access to a variety of reading material, they read more and enjoy it more. And children who read more outperform nonreaders on standardized tests.[13] Having books in the home has been correlated to higher test scores regardless of whether a child is read to by his parents. When he learned of this proven power of books, Illinois governor

Rod Blagojevich proposed mailing books to every child in the state every month from the time they were born until kindergarten, though the legislature rejected this ambitious $26 million plan.[14]

Another study found that books and libraries are even more important than teachers. Access to books and the time to read them are the most effective tools a teacher needs. "Books, not direct instruction, are key to vocabulary development."[15] The ability of students to browse library shelves freely and find books of interest is a vital component of academic success.

Libraries must remember that browsing is vital—and one advantage libraries have over online resources. Though remote storage is being forced on many libraries because of the lack of shelf space, the ability of users to peruse the shelves at leisure must be maintained. Even in this electronic age—perhaps as a direct result of it—people still benefit from the opportunity to just aimlessly wander the bookshelves in a library. Librarians should translate this need for shelf browsing into increased support for library buildings.

Beyond their practical benefits, books also carry an aura of reverence. Many religions incorporate books into their religious service because they are symbols of eternal knowledge and truth. Librarians can make a powerful case that, since books will not be going anywhere soon, we will continue to need adequate space for people to use them.

LIBRARIANS MUST DEMAND LIBRARIES SERVE AS COMMUNAL SPACE

Not only do people come to libraries seeking sanctuary and quiet, they also come to actually talk to each other. The informal schmoozing function provided by libraries is greatly undervalued. Libraries must reclaim their role as centers of the community. Not just public libraries, but all types of libraries can function as gathering spots for all members of the community that support the library. Starbucks and the major bookstore chains deliberately set out to create spaces that are a community's Third Place, usurping this role from public libraries. (The First Place is home, the Second is work; see chapter 7.) Libraries are Third Places as well, but they could capitalize on this fact to a greater extent by enhancing community-building programs and providing shared spaces.

The existence of a library proves that a community has come together to share resources among its members. Usually these shared resources are print, but often they include other items too expensive for each community member to own. Public access computers are good examples of such a shared communal resource. Because it is not feasible for each individual to have his or her own computer anywhere, anytime they need (at least not at this moment in computer development), the library provides them for sharing. As computers continue to decrease in size and cost, this shared need should decrease. If and when everyone has their own handheld computer that can access everything the library computer does, going to the library to use a computer will be as unheard of as going to a central "phone room" to make a call. Until that time, libraries will continue the role of providing shared computers. Though this service creates headaches for librarians—requiring procedures to manage time limits and to police game playing and e-mailing, not to mention demands for filtering software—libraries should remember and even celebrate that they have been given this difficult task. All of these problems are a direct result of fulfilling their function as a community resource.

Indeed, librarians may even want to seek out other resources too expensive or in short supply that could be shared by community members. (Did I just suggest that librarians give themselves more headaches?) Several libraries have experimented with toys, art reproductions, and laptop computers as shared resources.

One south Florida community experimented with a countywide event called the Free4All. This yard sale–like gathering invited everyone to bring unwanted items to a central spot. But rather than sell their wares, participants offered everything for free. Libraries may want to explore sponsoring such an activity as part of their community sharing mission.

Outrageously expensive textbooks are ripe for librarians to craft a creative way to share. Putting print textbooks on reserve is one way libraries already support this function, but surely there are other perhaps electronic means by which libraries could facilitate the sharing of these exorbitantly priced items. One idea would be for libraries to offer a central spot for students to exchange and sell their used textbooks, by far a preferred alternative to students taping hand-lettered signs to bathroom stalls. Or perhaps libraries could host a website for this purpose. Librarians excel at creating ways for community members to share resources, so they should easily be able to design other creative solutions to this problem.

Reading is, of course, one of the most basic communal activities libraries support. Though reading is usually engaged in privately, it carries profound social implications. When done alone, reading is a form of communication, though the person communicated with many not even be alive. When done as a group, in the form of a book discussion, reading can be a powerful social instrument bringing different people together for a common experience. One

Book/One Community programs are excellent examples of how libraries create community through books.

Librarians may wish to lend serious consideration to a fascinating proposal I once heard, though no one ever took it seriously. It was suggested—though I cannot credit any one source for the idea—that books intended for library circulation be published with several blank pages bound in the back of the book for reader comments. Building on the fact that libraries enable—and encourage—the passage of physical books from person to person, these blank pages would add to the process by allowing people's reactions to travel with the books at the same time. Much as the reader input section of Amazon.com encourages readers to share reviews online, this permanent record would enhance the exchange of ideas among readers via the book itself.

This simple publishing alteration could yield a fascinating new way for readers to communicate among themselves, but it would take some lobbying on the part of librarians and readers to be initiated. Since adding even blank pages to a book is expensive, publishers would need to be convinced that substantial benefits would derive from this addition. But if other library professionals find the idea as intriguing as I do, it could be done. Librarians could leverage their buying power by asking publishers to begin by adding blank reader pages to titles that circulate often and evoke reader comments. Library best-seller rental collections would be a good place to start, as would books intended for librarians, such as those published by ALA Editions. If successful, reader comment pages could be expanded to other subjects and collections that libraries purchase heavily. The simple addition of blank book pages could revolutionize book reviewing and bring an entirely new dimension to book discussion.

Imagine the time that could be saved if a cookbook came annotated with a handwritten comment in the back: "The double-chocolate brownies were excellent, but skip the chiffon cake." An English faculty member would have benefited greatly from such a system. He confessed to me that in high school he searched book pockets for the name of his mentor and would check out and read any he found. Imagine how his search would have been enhanced if the book also included comments from this esteemed individual, along with those of others who had read the volume.

LIBRARIANS MUST BALANCE LIBRARIES' PUBLIC AND PRIVATE FUNCTIONS

Book discussions are perfect examples of libraries combining two necessary, yet conflicting roles. To read a book, one needs silence. But to discuss a book, one needs to make noise—hopefully a lot of noise; ideally, book discussions should be punctuated with plenty of laughter and conducted with a chocolate chip cookie in one hand and a cup of coffee in the other. (Note: lively book discussions invariably come with spilled coffee.) The challenge before librarians is to find a way to balance these conflicting functions of library space.

Houses of worship experience the same conflicting needs but have done a better job designing buildings to accommodate them. Churches have glorious, awe-inspiring cathedrals that take your breath away and demand silence from even the most boisterous. But they also have homey social halls for people to gather, schmooze, eat, and, yes, spill. Libraries must find a way to offer spaces for serenity and socializing. Existing library buildings must be altered and new ones built to balance both lively chatter and silent, sacred space.

Some complain—rightly, in my opinion—that currently the social aspect of libraries has overtaken the contemplative nature of the institution. Some libraries have even taken on a carnival atmosphere. Somehow, libraries must maintain the lively social aspect of their mission but also support sanctuary and silence. The best way to do this would be to separate the two functions. Any new library building should provide users with a lofty, ethereal feeling of silent reverie and sanctuary among books. But at the same time it must provide ample community spaces, such as group study rooms, social halls, and lecture facilities. Little discussed but also central to this communal facilitation is the offering of food, a basic social enhancer in all cultures. Kitchens and food service equipment should be considered basic in any new building.

LIBRARIANS MUST CONTROL CHAOS

Along with speaking out about the need for libraries and books, librarians must continue to claim their roles as organizers and preservers of the written record of civilization. Librarians are uniquely qualified to organize, preserve, and tame the chaotic world of information. Ronald Reagan once said, "Status quo is Latin for the mess we're in," a perfect description of the current state of electronic information. The Internet has been likened to a library spilled on the floor. Attempts to organize the ocean of data could be imagined as sprinkling cards from a card catalog on top of the heap.

The situation is not only chaotic, it is even dangerous. Political theorist Yaron Ezrahi noted, "The diffusion of information through the Internet is more likely to transmit irrationality than rationality. Because irrationality is more emotionally loaded, it requires less knowledge, it explains more to more people, it goes down easier."[16] The kind of rational thought and contextual discussion found through books and articles is needed now more than ever. Libraries can provide rumor control by allowing people to dip into history for truth. Catalogers provide the key to the system that separates truth from fiction—both literally and figuratively.

Earlier in this book I acknowledged that libraries are not like hospitals. No one dies—at least directly—from bad service. But lives are affected nonetheless. Libraries and librarians lead people to the information, or entertainment, or wisdom, or knowledge they need. But they manage this feat only because the written record of civilization has been organized. Especially now, this organizational aspect of information is crucial. The value librarians add through controlled subject headings, indexed databases, and cataloging has not been appreciated. In many fields of study, library indexes are the only existing maps to a given body of knowledge.

Civilization could indeed be rebuilt through the preserved knowledge on the library shelves but only if the system of information control also survived. Academic research would come to a virtual standstill without an organized way to locate and access specific knowledge. Only through the system of library cataloging and classification could civilization hope to continue. Librarians must appreciate, and inform the public of, this vital role.

LIBRARIANS MUST TRUMPET THEIR ABILITY TO UPLIFT INDIVIDUALS AND SOCIETY

In contemporary American society, sin has been redefined as a personal failing that can be alleviated through individual self-improvement. Weight loss, healthy eating, loving relationships, financial success, academic achievement: these are among the paths people choose for salvation. Librarians are perfectly poised to assist with each of these redefined moral pursuits.

Along with individuals, society itself benefits from the institution of the library. Libraries are key players in enhancing democracy. Socrates defined justice as "the public and private state conductive to the good life"—an excellent definition of a library. It is no wonder that a librarian became a cultural hero in Iraq (see chapter 2). Her efforts to save books on the eve of that country's war were seen for what they were—an attempt to save the very fabric of that country's society.

When budget cuts threatened library branches, Philadelphia judge Matthew Carrafiello granted a stay to the sentence because, as he put it, "Libraries are a weapon in the arsenal against violence and drug use among youth." The cutbacks would endanger "the basic fabric of one of our most beloved Philadelphia institutions."[17]

Whatever the social problem, libraries can help devise a solution. Libraries have a long history of direct involvement in progressive social movements. Through the efforts of ALA, especially the Office for Intellectual Freedom, REFORMA, the Social Responsibilities Round Table, among others, libraries have been involved in various efforts to improve society. Granted, sometimes the proclamations of these bodies fall short of desired outcomes. As humanities librarian Eric Novotny put it, a gulf exists between "the idealistic rhetoric in the library literature and the actual results."[18] But librarians can take heart that, even in these cynical times, at least librarians remain idealistically optimistic.

Even when not directly involved in serving social causes, libraries hold within their midst the knowledge needed to craft a creative solution to any problem. Libraries literally prevent society from reinventing the wheel. Engineers, mathematicians, philosophers, and kings: no matter the person seeking or the problem to be solved, the shelves of the library contain the answer.

LIBRARIANS MUST REMEMBER THAT THEY TRANSMIT CULTURE AND IMMORTALITY

Libraries play a more active role in society than passively accumulating data. Arguably the most important resources libraries hold and pass on to future generations are stories. In an insightful book about the future of the industrialized world, Thomas Friedman argues that stories are central elements in the future of the human race. "Technology alone cannot keep us safe," he claims. "We need imagination—hopeful, life-affirming and tolerant imagination." And how does one develop imagination? Through stories. "Narratives that people are nurtured on—the stories and myths they and their religions and religious leaders tell themselves." These will save or destroy us in the future.[19]

And where are these stories recorded, organized, and passed on from one generation to the next? In the library, of course. Libraries are a natural place for this generation, and those of succeeding generations, to transmit their stories. Whether done through a preschool story hour or a teen book club or college library instruction class, libraries—much like religious traditions—hand down stories.

Libraries also lend an aura of immortality to those who use them. Libraries are one of the oldest continuing institutions in existence. Since words were first committed to paper (or parchment or tablets), libraries have preserved and transmitted the accumulated wisdom and knowledge of the ages. Library historian Matthew Battles concludes his survey of the thousand-year history of libraries by stating,

> The very fact that the library has endured seems to offer hope. In its custody of books and the words they contain, the library has confronted and tamed technology, the forces of change, the power of princes time and again. Librarians will continue to curate an abundance of books for some generations to come.[20]

Try to think of any other institution as long-lasting as the library. Hospitals were at one time imagined to be permanent, but they close or are bought and sold like any corporation. Colleges, likewise, come and go. Clifford Lynch predicts that some college libraries may even outlast their institution: "We may not need a physical academic place; but we need a physical library."[21]

SPIRITUALITY OF LIBRARIES AND FUND-RAISING

When I began writing this book, I did not intend it to be a justification for library fund-raising. But realizing the profound meaning of books and libraries in people's lives, I see that it can—and should—lead directly to financial gain for libraries. Too often librarians see fund-raising as a distasteful activity, one that "sells out" the purity of their activity. In their excellent book on library fund-raising, Victoria Steele and Stephen D. Elder report that librarians often explain, "We are people of the book, not of the checkbook," suggesting a fundamental incompatibility between librarianship and fund-raising.[22] But this attitude demonstrates a lack of understanding of both the basics of fund-raising and the meaning of libraries in people's lives. Rather than simply exploiting rich people, allowing those of means to support an institution or cause is actually doing them a favor. One nonprofit organization's fund-raiser explained, "I don't think of it as asking for money. I think of it as inviting people to participate."[23]

But those who support libraries derive something much more profound than just "participation." Giving to libraries provides donors an opportunity to identify with one of the most immortal of all institutions, thereby granting to themselves an imagined kind of immortality. Imagining one's memory or that of a loved one continuing beyond their physical time on earth is a powerful motivator for financial donors. As library director, I was twice handed unsolicited money for the library. Both times it was to honor the memory of a parent who had just died. In both instances the donors knew their gift would live on through the library because the library as an institution will continue.

Because imagined immortality is a large part of the motivation to give, libraries may want to concentrate their efforts on memorial gifts that will enable the person being remembered to live on. Research has shown that 90 percent of all giving comes from only 10 percent of donors.[24] Memorial gifts, which usually account for a large percentage of giving, are often given as an emotional and healing response to the death of a loved one. Since decisions about memorializing someone are sometimes made on the spur of the moment, libraries would benefit by making available an easy way to designate the library as the financial beneficiary through planned giving. For those who have not preplanned their giving, libraries may want to provide a method to designate the library as the source for memorial gifts, perhaps by working with funeral homes or newspaper obituary writers. The choice to designate the library, in lieu of flowers, could be suggested to those who had not earlier selected a recipient of memorial donations.

Beyond these memorial gifts, librarians should freely remind potential donors of the permanence represented by library giving. Especially now, in a world that appears to be spinning out of control with constant change, people need to affiliate with something that continues unchanged. Libraries give people affiliation with permanence.

SPIRITUALITY OF LIBRARIES AND LIBRARIAN RECRUITMENT

Finally, librarians must convey the spiritual aspect of their work to the next generation of librarians. The helping-guiding-teaching—yes, ministering—function of library service will continue to be needed in the future. When he founded the ALA, Melvil Dewey expressed "an intense faith in the future of libraries."[25] I too have faith, not only in the continuation of libraries but in the necessity of librarians to continue to render service to people. Writing this book has intensified my faith in the profession because of the quasi-religious nature of the librarian-patron interaction. When in need, some people turn to their spiritual leaders, but others head straight to the library.

Ironically, rather than replacing the library, the Internet often increases the need for the physical building. Many people go to the library to get help with their computers from a live person. Though online assistance is available, many prefer the patient, personal touch of the local librarian. Resembling how one consults a minister, in the library the person can admit their failings and seek both solace and answers (which may be why so many people approach the librarian with a confession of their ignorance). Whether the need is how to search by title or how to deal with a cancer diagnosis, help is available in an atmosphere of confidence and trust.

Despite the existence of online, time-zone-crossing reference assistance services, I predict that library assistance will continue to be conducted face-to-face, in person, between librarian and library user. When in need of a minister, few people turn to a computer service, though surely online access to clergy is available. Online college courses proliferate, but most people continue to attend classes in the traditional manner.

Though there surely is a role for certain kinds of information dispensing that can be provided online, I do not believe online access will replace the need for in-person library service. Predictions that everything will be replaced by online service remind me of the joke about a man who was planning to travel from California to Boston to visit his aged mother in a nursing home. "Why are you doing that?" asked his friend. "There are plenty of old ladies in nursing homes right here." Likewise, people seem to assume that just because one can communicate with people remotely, they will choose to do so, ignoring the very human aspect of in-person interactions.

In my opinion library reference service definitely qualifies as "nonfungible work," meaning "work that cannot be digitized or easily substituted." According to columnist Thomas L. Friedman, only this type of work will be performed in America in the future.[26]

Potential recruits to the profession will be reassured to learn that the need for this job will remain in the future. But they should also be reminded that the central mission of librarians is to help people. A commitment to serve draws and keeps people in the library field. "Service" is the operative word. When the name of the profession went from librarian to library scientist to information specialist, many worried that the emphasis on service would give way to technological know-how. Especially as the computer-savvy generation entered the field, many feared librarians would replace their commitment to service with access. But thankfully this has not occurred. Studies of new librarians reveal that they continue to enter the profession for the same reason their elders did: a desire to serve.[27] Likewise, dedication to service is what keeps seasoned librarians from leaving the field.

Much as the clergy feel called to serve through their religious institutions, librarians feel called to help by preserving, organizing, and uniting people with the written record of civilization known as the library. So vital is this role, heaven has been pictured as one huge Library in the Sky. What higher compliment could be paid to any institution than imaging it continuing through time immemorial? Librarianship is, indeed, the secular version of a sacred job. And, despite what teenagers may think, to become a librarian is no laughing matter.

NOTES

1. McGinn, "Myths."
2. As quoted in "Invest in the Future of Our Children and Our Community," Fort Lauderdale, FL: Broward Public Library Foundation brochure, n.d., 9.
3. As quoted in Durrance and Fisher, *How Libraries and Librarians Help*, 4.
4. "ALA Honors Jim Connor Trustee of Colorado PL," *Library Hotline*, April 18, 2005: 6.
5. Albanese, "Campus Library," 30.
6. As quoted in Edmundson, *Why Read?* 108.
7. Obama, "Bound to the Word," 52.
8. Pearl, "Lust for Reading," 35.
9. Lynch, "Future of Academic Libraries"; Sapp, *Brief History*, 51; Harris, *History of Libraries*, 293.
10. Sapp, *Brief History*, v–vi.
11. Ibid., 211.
12. Gorman, "Google and God's Mind."
13. Whitehead, " Effects of Increased Access."
14. Levitt and Dubner, *Freakonomics*, 172–73.
15. Shin, "Books, Not Direct Instruction," 20.
16. As quoted in Friedman, *World Is Flat*, 432.
17. "Judge Bars Philly Layoffs, Hours, Staff Downsizing," *Library Hotline*, April 18, 2005: 1.
18. Novotny, "Library Services to Immigrants."
19. Friedman, *World Is Flat*, 453.
20. Battles, *Library*, 212, 214.
21. Lynch, "Future of Academic Libraries."
22. Steele and Elder, *Becoming a Fundraiser*, 128.
23. As quoted in Olmeda, "Volunteer's Motto."
24. Steele and Elder, *Becoming a Fundraiser*, 2.
25. Sapp, *Brief History*, xi.
26. Friedman, *World Is Flat*, 238.
27. For more on service, see Sapp, *Brief History*, 207, 212.

Bibliography

Albanese, Andrew Richard. "Campus Library." *Library Journal*, April 15, 2004, 30.

American Library Association. "Number Employed in Libraries: ALA Library Fact Sheet 2." http://www.ala.org/ala/alalibrary/libraryfactsheet/alalibraryfact sheet2.htm.

Baker, Nicholson. *Double Fold: Libraries and the Assault on Paper*. New York: Vintage Books, 2001.

Banerjee, Tridib, and William C. Baer. *Beyond the Neighborhood Unit*. New York: Plenum Press, 1984.

Battelle, John. "The Birth of Google." *Wired*, August 2005, 103–6.

Battles, Matthew. *Library: An Unquiet History*. New York: Norton, 2003.

Bellah, Robert, et al. *Habits of the Heart*. Berkeley: University of California Press, 1985.

Benn, Evan S. "Dalai Lama in Davie Offers Advice, Gets Honorary Degree." *Miami Herald*, Sept. 19, 2004, 1–2B.

Besser, Howard. "The Future of Academic Libraries." American Library Association. Orlando, FL, June 27, 2004.

Black, Alistair. "From the Outside In: The Library in the Life of Its Historical Users." American Library Association. Orlando, FL, June 27, 2004.

Bloom, Harold. *How to Read and Why*. New York: Scribners, 2000.

Bostwick, Arthur E. *The American Public Library*. New York: D. Appleton, 1929.

Brisco, Shonda. "Dewey or Dalton? An Investigation of the Lure of the Bookstore." *Library Media Connection* 22 (Jan. 2004): 36–37.

Brooks, David. *On Paradise Drive*. New York: Simon and Schuster, 2004.

Cahill, Thomas. *The Gifts of the Jews*. New York: Nan A. Talese, 1998.

———. *How the Irish Saved Civilization*. New York: Doubleday, 1995.

Carroll, Jackson W., and Wade Clark Roof. *Bridging Divided Worlds: Generational Cultures in Congregations*. San Francisco: Jossey-Bass, 2002.

Cohen, Steven M. "Reader's Advisory: A Community Effort?" *Public Libraries* 44 (Jan./Feb. 2005): 24–25.

Cox, Harvey. *Common Prayers*. New York: Houghton Mifflin, 2001.

———. "The Market as God: Living in the New Dispensation." *Atlantic Monthly*, March 1999. http://www.theatlantic.com/issues/99mar/marketgod.htm.

———. *When Jesus Came to Harvard*. New York: Houghton Miflin, 2004.

Curran, Charles. "Two Models for Librarianship in the 1990s." *American Libraries*, March 1991, 254.

Davidman, Lynn. *Tradition in a Rootless World: Women Turn to Orthodox Judaism*. Los Angeles: University of California Press, 1991.

D'Elia, George, and Eleanor Jo Rodger. "Public Opinion about the Roles of the Public Library in the Community." *Public Libraries* 23 (Jan./Feb. 1994): 23–28.

Dewey, Melvil. *Abridged Dewey Decimal Classification and Relative Index*. 10th ed. New York: Forest Press, Lake Placid Club Education Foundation, 1971.

Douglas, W. Rae. *City*. New Haven, CT: Yale University Press, 2003.

Dowgiert, Diane. "The Spirituality of Science." October, 21 2001. First Unitarian Universalist Society of Marietta [Ohio]. http://www.fuusm.org/srm011021.htm.

Durrance, Joan C., and Karen E. Fisher. *How Libraries and Librarians Help*. Chicago: American Library Association, 2005.

Eck, Diana L. *A New Religious America*. San Francisco: HarperSanFrancisco, 2001.

Edmundson, Mark. *Why Read?* New York: Bloomsbury, 2004.

Forbes, Bruce David, and Jeffrey H. Mahan. *Religion and Popular Culture in America*. Berkeley: University of California Press, 2000.

Friedman, Thomas L. *World Is Flat*. New York: Farrar, Straus and Giroux, 2005.

Garrison, Dee. *Apostles of Culture: The Public Librarian and American Society, 1876–1920*. Madison: University of Wisconsin Press, 2003.

Gates, Henry Louis. *America Behind the Color Line*. New York: Warner Books, 2004.

Geertz, Clifford. *Interpretation of Cultures*. New York: Basic Books, 1973.

Goethals, Gregor T. *The TV Ritual: Worship at the Video Altar*. Boston: Beacon Press, 1981.

Gordon, Mary. *Shadow Man*. New York: Random House, 1996.

Gorman, Michael. "Google and God's Mind." *Los Angeles Times*, Dec. 17, 2004, B15.

Grafton, Anthony. *The Footnote: A Curious History*. Cambridge: Harvard University Press, 1997.

Grant, Don, Kathleen M. O'Neil, and Laura S. Stephens. 2003. "Neosecularization and Craft versus Professional Religious Authority in a Nonreligious Organization." *Journal for the Scientific Study of Religion* 42, no. 3 (2003): 479–87.

Greeley, Andrew M. *Religion as Poetry*. New Brunswick, NJ: Transaction, 1995.

Griliches, Diane Asseo. *Library: The Drama Within*. Albuquerque: University of New Mexico Press in Association with the Center for the Book in the Library of Congress, 1996.

Gunston, Robin. "Play Ball! How Sports Will Change in the 21st Century." *Futurist*, Jan./Feb. 2005, 31–36.

Hafner, Katie. "Old Search Engine, the Library, Tries to Fit into a Google World." *New York Times*, June 21, 2004, A16.

Harris, Michael H. *History of Libraries in the Western World*. 4th ed. Metuchen, NJ: Scarecrow Press, 1995.

Houdyshell, Mara, Patricia A. Robles, and Hua Yi. "What Were You Thinking: If You Could Choose Librarianship Again, Would You?" *Information Outlook*, July 3, 1999, 19–23.

Hunter, Gregory. *Developing and Maintaining Practical Archives*. New York: Neal Schuman, 1997.

Isaacson, David. "Sanctuary in Libraries." *American Libraries*, March 2004, 27.

Jacobsen, Teresa L. "Class of 1988." *Library Journal*, July 12, 2004, 38–41.

Jindra, Michael. "It's about Faith in Our Future," in Bruce David Forbes and Jeffrey H. Mahan, *Religion and Popular Culture in America*, 165–79. Berkeley: University of California Press, 2000.

Kaser, David. *The Evolution of the American Academic Library Building*. Lanham, MD: Scarecrow Press, 1997.

Kipnis, Laura. *Against Love: A Polemic*. New York: Pantheon, 2003.

Klein, Michele. *A Time to Be Born: Customs and Folklore of Jewish Birth*. Philadelphia: Jewish Publication Society, 1998.

Laderman, Gary. *Rest in Peace*. Oxford: Oxford University Press, 2003.

Lamott, Anne. *Plan B: Further Thoughts on Faith*. New York: Riverhead Books, 2005.

LaRue, James. "Buddha at the Gate, Running: Why People Challenge Library Materials." *American Libraries*, Dec. 2004, 42–44.

Leckie, Gloria J. "Three Perspectives on Libraries as Public Space." *Feliciter* 50, no. 6 (2004): 233–36.

Lerner, Betsy. *Forest for the Trees*. New York: Riverhead Books, 2000.

Levitt, Steven D., and Stephen J. Dubner. *Freakonomics: A Rogue Economist Explores the Hidden Side of Everything*. New York: William Morrow, 2005.

Lipson, Eden Ross. "Iraqi Librarian Becomes Cultural Hero in 2 Children's Books." *New York Times*, Mar. 17, 2005, B3.

Lynch, Clifford. "The Future of Academic Libraries." American Library Association. Orlando, FL, June 27, 2004.

Magdalinski, Tara, and Timothy J. L. Chandler, eds. *With God on Their Side: Sport in the Service of Religion.* New York: Routledge, 2002.

Mandel, Peter. "Once Upon a Time, Silence Was Golden." *Sun-Sentinel* (Ft. Lauderdale, FL), Oct. 12, 2004, 23A.

Manguel, Alberto. *A History of Reading.* New York: Viking, 1996.

Maxwell, Nancy Kalikow. "Final Touches." *Reform Judaism Magazine* 29, no. 3 (2001): 53–56.

———. "A Nice Jewish Girl Studying Catholicism?" *National Catholic Reporter* 9 (April 2004): 19.

———. "Seven Deadly Sins of Library Technology." *American Libraries,* Sept. 2004, 40–42.

Mazur, Eric Michael, and Kate McCarthy. *God in the Details: American Religion in Popular Culture.* New York: Routledge, 2001.

McCabe, Ronald B. *Civic Librarianship.* Lanham, MD: Scarecrow Press, 2001.

McElroy, John Harmon. *American Beliefs.* Chicago: Ivan R. Dee, 1999.

McGinn, Howard F. "Myths, Missionary Expeditions and Mobilizing the Profession." *Versed,* May/June 2005, 6. http://www.ala.org/ala/diversity/versed/versedbackissues/may2005abcd/mythsnmobilizing.htm.

Milton, Pat. "Urban Lions Fortitude, Patience Undergo Face-Lift." *Sun-Sentinel* (Ft. Lauderdale, FL), Nov. 19, 2004, 10A.

Mirvis, Tova. *Outside World.* New York: Knopf, 2004.

Molotch, Harvey. *Where Stuff Comes From.* New York: Routledge, 2003.

Moore, Timothy. "Myers-Briggs Type Indicator." *Gale Encyclopedia of Psychology.* 2d ed. New York: Gale Group, 2001.

Morkes, Andrew, ed. *Encyclopedia of Careers and Vocational Guidance.* 12th ed. Vol. 4. Chicago: Ferguson, 2003.

Morris, Raymond P. "Theological Librarianship as a Ministry." June 11, 1953. http://www.ptsem.edu/grow/library/nyatla/PDFdocs/morris.pdf.

Moyers, Bill. *Moyers on America.* New York: New Press, 2004.

Myerberg, Henry. "School Libraries: A Design Recipe for the Future." *Knowledge Quest* 31, no. 1 (2002): 11–13.

Nathanson, Paul. *Over the Rainbow: The Wizard of Oz as a Secular Myth of America.* Albany: State University of New York Press, 1991.

National Jewish Population Survey 2000–01 (Electronic data file). New York United Jewish Communities [Producer]. Waltham, MA: North American Jewish Data Bank [Distributor], 2003.

Neilson, Robert E., and Debra Stouffer. "Narrating the Vision: Scenarios in Action." *Futurist,* May–June 2005, 26–30.

Newhouse, Ria, and April Spisak. "Fixing the First Job." *Library Journal*, Aug. 2004, 44–46.

Novotny, Eric. "Library Services to Immigrants: The Debate in the Literature, 1900–1920, and a Chicago Case Study." *Reference & User Services Quarterly* 42, no. 4 (2003): 342–52.

Obama, Barack. "Bound to the Word." *American Libraries*, Aug. 2005, 49–52.

Oldenburg, Ray. *The Great Good Place.* New York: Paragon House, 1989.

Olmeda, Rafael A. "Volunteer's Motto: It Never Hurts to Ask—for a Lot." *Sun-Sentinel* (Ft. Lauderdale, FL), June 3, 2005, 3B.

Onwuegbuzie, Anthony J., Qun G. Jiao, and Sharon L. Bostick. *Library Anxiety: Theory, Research, and Applications.* Lanham, MD: Scarecrow Press, 2004.

Ostwalt, Conrad. *Secular Steeples: Popular Culture and the Religious Imagination.* Harrisburg, PA: Trinity Press, 2003.

Pagels, Elaine. *Beyond Belief: The Secret Gospel of Thomas.* New York: Random House, 2003.

Pahl, Jon. *Shopping Malls and Other Sacred Spaces: Putting God in Place.* Grand Rapids, MI: Brazos Press, 2003.

Palmer, Parker J. *A Hidden Wholeness: The Journey toward an Undivided Life.* San Francisco: Jossey-Bass, 2004.

———. *To Know as We Are Known: Education as a Spiritual Journey.* San Francisco: HarperSanFrancisco, 1993.

Pawley, Christine. "Reading Apostles of Culture: The Politics and Historiography of Library History," in Dee Garrison, *Apostles of Culture: The Public Librarian and American Society, 1876–1920*, xvii–xxix. Madison: University of Wisconsin Press, 2003.

Pearl, Nancy. "Lust for Reading." *American Libraries* 36, no. 5 (2005): 32–36.

Peltz, Jennifer. "Faculty Assigned Summer Reading." *Sun-Sentinel* (Ft. Lauderdale, FL), July 12, 2004, 1B.

Pevsner, Nikolaus. *A History of Building Types.* Princeton, NJ: Princeton University Press, 1976.

Porterfield, Amanda. *The Transformation of American Religion.* New York: Oxford University Press, 2001.

Prothero, Stephen. *American Jesus: How the Son of God Became a National Icon.* New York: Farrar, Straus and Giroux, 2003.

Putnam, Robert D. *Bowling Alone: The Collapse and Revival of American Community.* New York: Simon and Schuster, 2000.

Rippel, Chris. "What Public Libraries Can Learn from Superbookstores." *Australasian Public Libraries and Information Services* 16, no. 4 (2003): 147–55.

Roberts, Sam. *Who We Are Now*. New York: Times Books, 2004.

Roof, Wade Clark. "Blood in the Barbecue?" in Eric Michael Mazur and Kate McCarthy, *God in the Details: American Religion in Popular Culture*, 100–122. New York: Routledge, 2001.

———. *Generation of Seekers*. New York: HarperSanFrancisco, 1993.

Rosen, Jonathan. *Joy Comes in the Morning*. New York: Farrar, Straus and Giroux, 2004.

———. *Talmud and the Internet*. New York: Farrar, Straus and Giroux, 2000.

Sapp, Gregg. *A Brief History of the Future of Libraries: An Annotated Bibliography*. Lanham, MD: Scarecrow Press, 2002.

Saunders, Michelle. "The Young Adult OutPost: A Library Just for Teens." *Public Libraries* 42, no. 2 (2003): 113–16.

Schwartz, Barry. *Paradox of Choice*. New York: HarperCollins, 2004.

Schwartz, Howard. *Tree of Souls: The Mythology of Judaism*. New York: Oxford University Press, 2004.

Shin, Fay. "Books, Not Direct Instruction, Are the Key to Vocabulary Development." *Library Media Connection*, Jan. 2004, 20–21.

Skenazy, Lenore. "When Skinny Means Happy." *Miami Herald*, June 12, 2004, 21A.

Skocpol, Theda. *Diminished Democracy: From Membership to Management in American Civic Life*. Norman: University of Oklahoma Press, 2003.

Slone, D. Jason. *Theological Incorrectness*. New York: Oxford University Press, 2004.

Smith, Dinitia. "Demonizing Fat in the War on Weight." *New York Times*, May 1, 2004, A15–A17.

Solomon, Andrew. "Closing of the American Book." *New York Times*, July 10, 2004, A29.

Steckel, Mike. "Ranganathan for IA's." http://www.boxesandarrows.com/archives/ranganathan_for_ias.php.

Steele, Victoria, and Stephen D. Elder. *Becoming a Fundraiser: The Principles and Practice of Library Development*. 2d ed. Chicago: American Library Association, 2000.

Sterling, Bruce. "The Evolution Will Be Mechanized." *Wired*, Sept. 2004, 102.

Susman, Warren I. *Culture as History: The Transformation of American Society in the Twentieth Century*. New York: Pantheon Books, 1984.

Thompson, Lawrence S. "Scriptoria," in *Encyclopedia of Library and Information Science*. Vol. 27, 146–47. New York: Marcel Dekker, 1979.

Tolzmann, Don Heinrich, Alfred Hessel, and Reuben Peiss. *The Memory of Mankind: The Story of Libraries since the Dawn of History*. New Castle, DE: Oak Knoll Press, 2001.

Tvaruzka, Kati. "Teen Lounge: L. E. Phillips Memorial Public Library, Eau Claire, Wisconsin. 2003." *Voice of Youth Advocates* 26, no. 4 (2003): 294–95.

Underhill, Paco. *Call of the Mall*. New York: Simon and Schuster, 2004.

U.S. Census Bureau. "Employed Civilians by Occupation, Sex, Race, and Hispanic Origin: 1983 and 2002." *Statistical Abstract of the U.S.* Washington, DC: U.S. Government Printing Office, 2003. http://www.census.gov/prod/www/statistical-abstract-1995_2000.html.

Wheatley, Margaret J. *Turning to One Another*. San Francisco: Berrett-Koehler, 2002.

Whitehead, Nicole. "The Effects of Increased Access to Books on Student Reading Using the Public Library." *Reading Improvement* 41, no. 3 (2004): 165–78.

Whitfield, Stephen J. *In Search of American Jewish Culture*. Hanover, NH: Brandeis University Press, University Press of New England, 1999.

Wiegand, Wayne A. "Critiquing the Curriculum." *American Libraries*, Jan. 2005: 58–61.

Willingham, Taylor. "Interview: Straight Answers from Taylor Willingham." *American Libraries*, April 2005, 23.

Wolfe, Alan. *The Transformation of American Religion: How We Actually Live Our Faith*. New York: Free Press, 2003.

Woocher, Jonathan S. *Sacred Survival: The Civil Religion of American Jews*. Bloomington: Indiana University Press, 1986.

Index

Nancy Kalikow Maxwell has written extensively on library and religion topics, with contributions to *American Libraries*, *National Catholic Reporter*, *Tikkun*, *Lilith*, and *Reform Judaism* among others. She holds master's degrees in library science from the University of Missouri–Columbia and in Catholic theology from Barry University and has more than thirty years of professional library experience in public and academic libraries. Currently an administrator at Miami Dade College North Campus Library, Maxwell lives in the Fort Lauderdale area with her husband and daughter. She can be reached at

nancymaxwell@bellsouth.net.